STANLEY GIBBONS

A Birmingham student decided on a career in Education, Head of Science in secondary schools in Staffordshire, Southern Rhodesia and Berkshire. Chief Examiner in Rural Studies for the Southern Region Examination Board.

In 1967 created in an empty New Forest school an Environmental Studies Centre for Hampshire schools on both day and residential basis. The varied Forest habitats were the workshops for pupils to investigate flora and fauna leading to a respect for living things and care for the environment.

Chairman in 1980 of the National Association for Environmental Education.

Retiring in 1991 devoted more time to Beekeeping, taught beekeeping classes: chair of New Forest Association and served Hampshire Federation as chairman and president.

Happily married to Gillian since 1957: one son and two daughters: interests include horticulture, photography, classical music and travel.

MINSTEAD

50 YEARS
and
COUNTING

A New Forest Village
Through The Eyes Of One Man

Stanley Gibbons

Matador
9 Priory Business Park,
Wistow Road, Kibworth Beauchamp,
Leicestershire. LE8 0RX
Tel: 0116 279 2299
Email: books@troubador.co.uk
Web: www.troubador.co.uk/matador
Twitter: @matadorbooks

ISBN 978 1789018 561

British Library Cataloguing in Publication Data.
A catalogue record for this book is available from the British Library.

Printed and bound by CPI Group (UK) Ltd, Croydon, CR0 4YY
Typeset in 11pt Minion Pro by Troubador Publishing Ltd, Leicester, UK

Matador is an imprint of Troubador Publishing Ltd

I dedicate this story to my

children –

Sandra, John and Jane

who grew up in this

New Forest village

CONTENTS

CONTENTS

ILLUSTRATIONS

ILLUSTRATIONS

PREFACE

Stanley and Gillian Gibbons were among the first people to make us welcome when we came to Minstead in 1996 and we have been neighbours and good friends ever since.

It quickly became obvious that Stanley had amazingly clear recall, especially of detail as is evident in this book.

Both Stanley and Gillian contributed to and participated hugely in Minstead Village life – in Church, School, Parish Council, Training Project and Junior Minstead to name but a few.

I am honoured and delighted to commend this book to you.

Bill Andrews
Chairman
Parish Council

FOREWORD

This fascinating book by Stanley Gibbons recounts his development of the Rural Studies Centre in Minstead and his own memories of this beautiful village over 50 years. However, it is also much more than that. Although he is too modest to say so, it is plain that the Studies Centre made an enormous difference to the lives of children in Hampshire over the period he ran it - one boy said "Wouldn't it be lovely if the next school cancelled their visit and we could stay here next week?"

His wide knowledge of the Forest and its history and origins were central to the success of the Centre, and he provides fascinating vignettes of the kind of activities visiting children were offered; from watching the deer, to identifying 'bugs' under the microscope, to feeding the hens, rabbits and the famous geese, Charles and Petunia. For some children, this was their first time out of their estate, and the experience must have been life-changing for them. The beauty and complexity of this extraordinary area is made clear as well as the author's deep knowledge and love of the New Forest.

However, the success of the Centre did not come easily; Gillian Gibbons ran the domestic side of the Centre, as well as looking after their three children, and the courses were carefully prepared for. Open days helped to sell the experience to many and all teachers went on a day course to prepare them and help their pupils get the most out of the week of residence. Success had to be worked for, but what is moving about his account of the Rural Studies Centre is his ability to get children to notice what is around them, and even more important, to begin to understand its delicate complexity. The importance of conservation was made clear to those lucky students and Stanley Gibbons was clearly ahead of his time in emphasising our interdependence with nature.

But this book is not just about the Rural Studies Centre. Stanley Gibbons recounts his memories of the New Forest, and Minstead in particular, over the last fifty years – from the fascinating medieval organisation of Foresters, commoners' rights of pannage and turbary, to the saga of the Church bells and the changing face of Minstead. He is able to tell stories about the lives of the village boys in 1905 - bringing the cows in before school and the long journeys to market with produce to sell. The village, like all living places, has changed hugely, yet remains the same. Stanley Gibbons' book is part of our national story which is built up and woven in with these countless, precious local stories and memories, and he has played a vital role here, both in his participation in those events, and in his outstanding ability to communicate these memories so vividly. This book will be treasured by all those who are lucky enough to live in Minstead and the New Forest, and all those who wish they could.

Emily Spence

CHAPTER 1

THE NEW FOREST

One Sunday afternoon in August 1966 – I had left my house and family in Wantage and was driving southwards on the A34 Trunk Road in my beloved Midnight Grey coloured M.G.ZB Magnette saloon car, one of the last to be exported to Africa from the factory in Abingdon-on-Thames.

Arriving in Winchester I turned right at the cross-roads near the centre of the city, went up the hill past The Castle, through the big stone archway, driving on the A31 Trunk Road towards Cadnam on the edge of the New Forest.

At the Cadnam round-about I turned southwards over a cattle-grid on to the road leading to Lyndhurst. Warning notices advised drivers that animals could be met wandering over the road.

I was heading for Emery Down near Lyndhurst. At the T-junction in Lyndhurst I turned right up the hill past the Church towards Emery Down. My destination was Northerwood House: there were no signs to it. I pulled into the petrol-filling station adjoining the Swan pub to fill up with petrol and seek directions.

Crossing the main A35 Lyndhurst to Christchurch road, I drove past the white-clad cricketers playing on the Swan Green Cricket Club pitch. On the brow of the hill: on the right-hand side was a large entrance with a notice board – Northerwood House.

The white entrance gates were pegged back: crossing the gateway cattle grid I drove along a long winding driveway lined

New Forest Pony

Road Sign

with shrubs and tall trees and round a final bend to the large courtyard parking area in front of Northerwood House. This large imposing mansion was owned by the Forestry Commission and was their residential education centre.

Why had I come here? During 1965 I had become aware that each August the Forestry Commission ran a very popular week-long course beamed specifically at people in the world of education, the purpose to introduce them to the world of Woodland and Forestry. This was one aspect of my educational profile that was deficient. I knew that numbers on the course were limited so I applied for the 1966 course during the previous November so as to be early in the queue!

Parking my car I then walked through the oak-framed double doorway into the large entrance hall: the walls were clad in dark oak panelling and a grand staircase led up to landings on the two floors above.

High on the walls of the entrance hall were mounted a number of Army Regimental Plaques each stating when they had occupied the mansion as headquarters during the 1939-1945 War.

I checked in at the desk near the entrance and was shown the oak doors leading to the main dining room, the lecture hall, and a lounge where tea and biscuits would be available at 4.30pm. Dinner would be at 7pm: we would be summoned by the huge gong in the entrance hall. In the meantime I was to make myself at home!

Collecting my gear from the car I went up the grand staircase to the first-floor bedroom that I was to share with a man from Wiltshire.

I opened the door to the room at the front of the building in the East Wing – WOW! A large room with two large single beds, wardrobes, lockers, bed-side tables. Two large windows faced southwards – the view, over the Forest to the Isle-of-Wight!

Tea and biscuits in the lounge: there was a small bar here that would be opened before dinner. We were told that the

West wing was closed: cracks had appeared at the end due to subsidence. The resident domestic staff lived up on the second floor.

Walking round the outside of the mansion showed that it had been built on the top of a small hill. At the front, south side, the land fell away steeply: a narrow belt of mature trees grew at the base of the slope but they did not impede the view from the mansion over the Forest.

The long building had the appearance of being flat-roofed: it was painted white and was very distinctive.

The gong sounded! Entering the Dining Hall we were greeted by the Forestry Officer who was overseeing our course. He introduced us to Head Forester John Middleton who would be with us all week: he lived in the Lodge near the entrance gates.

Seated at the long table we were waited on by male waiters dressed in starched white jackets and wearing white gloves. A substantial four-course meal was followed by coffee and mints. The domestic arrangements were outlined by John Middleton.

Breakfast would be served from 7.15am. Our beds would be made and our rooms cleaned during the morning: beds would be turned-down at tea-time. This really was like a FOUR-STAR hotel!

In the lecture room at 9.00am the structure of our course was outlined by the Forestry Officer. Each day there would be a talk or demonstration in the lecture room at 9.00am. After coffee we would be taken by minibus to see the many aspects of forestry that were practised in the New Forest: a packed lunch would be provided.

Dinner would be followed by a talk.

* * *

The Forestry Commission had been created by the Government in the early 1920s. Its purpose was to grow plantations of timber trees, especially softwoods, on Crown lands and other land throughout the British Isles so that in the future the nation would be less dependent upon imported timber. The bulk of their operations was on higher land in the northern half of the British Isles.

He then outlined the structure of the Forestry Commission in the New Forest. The headquarters was in the Queen's House in Lyndhurst. Here were the administrative staff who worked under the chief forestry officer who was known as "The Deputy Surveyor": he was assisted by District Forestry Officers – they were all university forestry graduates.

The technical grade staff who are responsible for the practicalities of growing and harvesting trees are the Foresters. A Head Forester for each district and one Chief Forester for the whole forest.

Auxilliary staff were employed to do planting, fencing, estate carpentry etc. A range of houses and cottages were allocated to all the grades of staff.

Sub-contractors were used to do tree felling.

Each district had a Keeper who was a wildlife officer with one Head Keeper for the whole forest: they lived in Keepers Cottages.

* * *

Head Forester John Middleton took over the remainder of the session armed with a bucket of tree twigs, each about a foot long.

We each had twigs of the hardwood trees, oaks and beeches and of the softwoods, larches, pines and firs that were grown in the forest. We learned their habit, leaf recognition, the ways the different species produced seeds and the uses of their timber.

He would ask us to recognise them in the forest!

Coffee time, then geared up to get in the mini-buses to drive to forest sites to "meet the trees".

During the week we were taken to see a plantation of mature oaks planted during the times of the Napoleonic Wars period to ensure future supplies of naval timber and to see plantations of softwood trees including Larch, Spruce and Pine.

Starting at Bolderwood we followed the narrow road southwards through sections of the Ornamental Drive to see the great Knightwood Oak, the oldest pollarded oak in the Forest. Crossing the A35 we continued along the Ornamental Drive past the stand of huge Douglas fir trees, planted in 1859 on past Rheinfield House to Brockenhurst.

We visited Buckler's Hard and learned about the naval sailing ships that had been constructed here from Forest timber including HMS Swiftsure and HMS Euryalus during the early 1800s.

* * *

A journey westwards along the single-carriageway A31 trunk road to the tree nursery in Ringwood Forest where varieties of softwood species were sown and reared on sandy soil.

In another area we watched large trees being felled by sub-contractors who were clear-felling old mixed woodland that was to be used for a new softwood plantation. They were using motor-saws that had recently come on the market: this greatly increased their productivity, a fact that was not being recognised financially by the Forestry Commission!

* * *

During talks we learned history: how the Norman Conquerors had taken over this natural woodland – Ytene, reputedly settled by the Jutes – and established it as a New Royal Hunting Forest.

The local inhabitants were not allowed to have any fences or barriers that would impede the flight of the deer or their pursuing huntsmen!

To compensate them there evolved over time certain Forest Rights for the locals, now known as The Commoners: these Rights still exist today.

The Right of Pannage allows depasturing of ponies, cattle and donkeys on open forest land.

The Right of Mast allows pigs to be turned on to open forest to eat acorns and beech mast for a period of 60 days during Autumn. The actual dates are decided each year by the authorities.

The Right of Estovers or Attachment gives cords of firewood.

The Right of Turberry permits the cutting of turf for fuel, a Right seldom used.

Nowadays these Rights are vested not in people but in properties or pieces of land in the Forest: the owners of these are listed: they are The Commoners and have the right to vote in the election of their representatives – The Verderers.

* * *

A visit to Queen's House then to the adjacent older building next door, the Verderers Court. Raised at the rear of the room was a long wooden bench where the Verderers sat. On the wall behind them was a large Royal Emblem that remained from the last Court of Assize held here when Lord Chief Justice came to try local folk who had committed serious offences: an accused person stood in the dock at a lower level before the Justice – the dock is still there. The Court of Assize was held once or twice a year.

Nowadays the Verderers Court, that meets on Mondays bi-monthly dispenses justice on breaches of Forest Law (rules). As well as the five Verderers elected by the Commoners there are four appointed Verderers – one each by the Forestry Commission, Hampshire County Council, the Ministry of Agriculture, and the Countryside Commission.

The Verderers employ a number of Agisters whose job is to oversee the Commoners animals on the open forest and to collect the annual fee for each animal.

On one wall of the Verderers Hall were several mounted animal heads including the famous Fallow deer "The Great White Buck of Burley".

On the wall was also a replica of a large Norman rider's stirrup. If a Commoners dog could not crawl through the stirrup then it was considered large enough to be a danger to the Norman King's deer: it would have to be "expeditated", i.e. all the claws on its two front feet were removed so that it would be unable to bring down a deer!

* * *

In the lecture room we met a senior Agister: he was wearing the distinctive uniform that had to be worn at all meetings of the Verderers Court – green jacket, riding breeches, and leather gaiters with a green hard hat bearing the insignia of the Verderers Stirrup.

To be appointed he had to have an intimate knowledge of the large areas of woodland, moor and bog in his area or "beat". He had to be a good horseman able to gallop over rough terrain.

Duties included keeping an eye on the condition of all the ponies on his beat, attending all animal road casualties and organising the annual pony round-up or "drift" where the ponies were rounded up and corralled, by the owners. Using the system of gates at these stations each pony had a new ear tag inserted to show the annual Verderers' fee had been paid. At the same time the Agister cut the pony's tail in the particular pattern of the "beat" – a more visible sign that the fee had been paid. The term Agister is an old Norman term meaning "collector of fees".

At this time some owners branded ponies, especially young ones being licensed to be on the Forest as an adult for the first time. Each pony owner had their own brand mark, several hundred distinctive marks over the whole Forest.

During a hard winter some ponies lost physical condition: then the Agister gets the owner to take them off the Forest and have them on the pasture fields of his own holding for care and feeding of hay.

All in all, as well as running his own Commoner's holding this Agister has a very varied and interesting job – never a spare moment!

* * *

In our free time we went to sample the ales at the Swan Inn and walked down into Lyndhurst High Street where the traffic travelled in both directions whilst avoiding the ponies. Horses ridden up the street went through a large archway into the stables opposite Lloyds Bank. Next to the bank was a greengrocery shop with trays of produce stacked outside: a pony stole a cabbage and was chased down the street by the greengrocer!

Lower down that side of the street was a petrol pump outside a garden machinery shop. At the bottom of the High Street was a garage with petrol pumps.

A busy village delighting in the title – "The Capital of the New Forest".

* * *

On the last evening we had a talk by the Deputy Surveyor, Mr Arthur Cadman. With the aid of many slide transparencies projected on to a screen he described the lives of many of the wild animals that inhabited the Forest. Badgers built extensive "setts" in sandy hillsides but they were suffering road deaths during their lengthy nocturnal journeyings.

Grey Squirrels, a 19th Century import from North America had caused the disappearance of the native Red Squirrel from the Forest. The Greys caused much damage to young plantation trees. Each winter teams of Keepers and Foresters held organised "Squirrel shoots" when the "dreys" were poked with long poles.

Of the three types of native deer in the Forest, the Red, the largest yet least numerous, are found in the northern half, whilst the Fallow and Roe are widely distributed. Small herds of Japanese Sika deer are found south of the Southampton to Bournemouth railway line that traverses the Forest.

All the male deer "cast" or shed their bony antlers in the Spring. Old antlers on the Forest floor are one of the Keepers perks. During the Summer new antlers grow from "buds" on the top of the head. They are protected by a velvety fur that nourishes them. In late summer the new antlers are fully grown, the "velvet" dries up and the deer rub their new antlers on trunks of trees to get rid of the irritating old velvet so leaving striations on the trunk. New antlers are rubbed on trees in order to harden the bone ready for possible fighting in the Autumn mating or rutting season.

The Fallow does give birth to their fawns usually in long grass: they eat the "after-birth" and lick their fawns all over so as to reduce their attraction to foxes. They go to nearby dense brush cover. Visitors often report these fawns as abandoned and some pick them up and bring them to the Commission having "rescued them." Left alone the doe will visit the fawn periodically to suckle it!

Deer, as well as eating ground level pasturage, will also browse leaves off trees – they leave visible "browse lines" at the limit of their reach.

Mr Cadman related a story. One day in his office in the Queen's House he was listening to a complainant. The man was getting nowhere so he said that as I was only the deputy so he wished to see The Surveyor. I told him he would have to go to

London to Buckingham Palace for THE SURVEYOR was the Queen!

The course ended on the Saturday morning. I had been persuaded to give the vote of thanks to all the staff for the wonderful tuition and hospitality that had been given to us at Northerwood House.

Lunch, the goodbyes and the journey home.

The New Forest has about 140 square miles of land within its "Perambulation" or boundary: this includes many villages and settlements.

It is a captivating area with its interesting historical past and such a range of Natural History.

Must come again one day!

The Author 1967

CHAPTER 2

ITCHY FEET

January 1967 and I was in my seventh year as head of a large department in a Berkshire secondary school. From a professional point of view I thought that it was time to make a move in the educational world.

I started to buy the weekly edition of the Times Educational Supplement where senior post vacancies were advertised.

Mid-January and my wife Gillian had spotted a particular advertisement that she pointed out to me when I came home on the Friday teatime: it was a large feature advertisement on the top of the back cover page.

"Look at this! It is what you have been preaching to me ever since I met and married you in Rhodesia!"

Hampshire County Council were intending to set up a Studies Centre for pupils up to the age of 14 years in an empty school in The New Forest. They required someone to create it.

Yes – it would be a challenge, something quite different. The weekend was spent drafting my application that was posted on the Monday together with copies of my credentials, etc and names of referees. A few days later I received an acknowledgement from Winchester. The weeks went by – nothing. NOT FOR ME!

* * *

I still had wanderlust and an itch to travel. Australia and New Zealand had always had an appeal. At the end of the year my eldest child would be six years old, young enough to be assimilated into either country without standing out and being victimised as a POMME!

During February half-term I went to London for interview at Tasmania House. I was offered a post as Head of a Country School in Tasmania – up to 14 years of age, to start work in January 1968. I accepted the post!

Easter holiday saw me interviewed in Oxford by the New Zealand Chief Inspector of Schools. I was offered a post for January 1968 as Head of Science at Hamilton High School, North Island. This I accepted!

A Friday morning in mid May and an envelope arrived from Hampshire County Council inviting me to attend The Castle the next Friday for interview for the New Forest post!

The next day, Saturday, we all set off early in our MG Magnette for Minstead in the New Forest. Arriving at the Village Green we looked for the school – the Old Technical School? Can't be that! To the Village Shop and got directions to the locked up empty school overlooking the dry ford at Fleetwater.

A careful walk around the buildings and the site making notes in my field notebook. Then a drive around the area that led to a picnic lunch on the wide road verge on the Emery Down to Robinsbush Road nearly opposite the signposted entrance to Minstead Manor.

Then two hours ranging around the area making notes in my field note book before making the return journey to Wantage.

Next Friday, the family parked with neighbours for the day, Gillian and I drove down to Winchester. Lunch at a half-timbered restaurant, then a walk up the hill to the Castle.

There were three other couples for interview: there was a part-time auxiliary post for the wife to oversee the domestic arrangements at the Centre.

We were last to be called in for interview. After an interval, Gillian and I were called back into the interview room. The Deputy Director of Education, Mr Birtwistle, barrister-at-law, offered us the post, to start on the 1st of September: we accepted!

We drove back to Wantage on that Bank Holiday Friday teatime knowing that we had decisions to make.

Would we go to The New Forest, take the children to the Antipodes or stay at the school that I enjoyed in Wantage where we had a wide circle of friends many of whom were at the nearby Harwell Atomic Research Establishment?

Sunday came: we had made our decision – The New Forest had won! I wrote my letter of resignation to my employees, the Royal County of Berkshire: this had to be in by the end of the month.

Letters were written to Tasmania House and New Zealand House in London and were posted on the Monday.

Now we could sit back, relax and enjoy the half-term week's holiday with the children!

* * *

Tuesday morning, 9.00am the phone rang. The Education Offices, Winchester. Mr Crowfoot, a senior administrative officer, to speak to me. He was going down to the empty school at Minstead tomorrow accompanied by Mr Swindlehurst, the Sites and Building Officer, to decide what minor alterations had to be budgeted for. Could I go down there and meet them on site at 10.00am the next day, Wednesday, so as to make my input into their decisions?

Wednesday morning and the long drive via the A34 and A31 to Minstead School: the two gentlemen were there to meet me. Mr Leslie Crowfoot explained that the Studies Centre project had been delayed by lack of funds. In late April they had squeezed a small amount from another source, enough to allow the project to proceed. However finances were very tight during the rest of the financial year so any alterations would have to be very limited.

Old Technical School

Plaque

The School House was still being rented by the last teacher to have been at the school before closure. However she was under notice to leave by the end of term. We had full access to the school as they had been given the keys by the part-time caretaker who still kept an eye on the property.

The school had two classrooms separated by a high movable folding wooden screen that could be moved back to create one large teaching space. The end room, the smaller, had been the Infants room with an entrance porch from the yard which had coat pegs and two wash basins with running cold water.

The larger room had a separate entrance porch from the yard, again with coat pegs and two wash basins. This larger classroom had a large free-standing iron solid fuel burning stove sitting on a concrete base near the wall nearest the School House.

A door from the large classroom led to a room that had been used as the school office, a room that had once been a sitting room of the School House: there were bedrooms above it and a door, now locked, led into the House hallway where there was a flushing toilet.

Another room, entered from the back yard had been taken from the house to provide a school kitchen. It was thought that there were cellars under the house.

* * *

Toilets for the children were at the top of the yard; three sit-down flushing toilets for the girls, two for the boys plus a urinal by which was a free-standing cold water pipe loosely bracketed to the wall.

All effluent from the toilet was piped underground to a cess pit hidden in the front garden shrubbery of the School House.

Adjoining the toilet block was an open-fronted lean-to shed. From there a door led to several steep steps into a wide brick-walled "room" or space that extended the whole length of the toilet block: it was covered by the backward extension of the toilet block roof and there was another door into it at the far end.

Prior to the advent of flushing toilets and the cess pit, all the toilet waste fell through into this "room" (space) and was absorbed by a deep layer of sawdust and chopped straw. Every holiday this effluent mixture was removed from site by horse-and-cart to be spread on a smallholder's field.

* * *

On the yard next to the lean-to was a large free-standing wooden garage that was used by the Head-teacher.

During the next two hours discussion led to decisions being made:

- the infants' entrance would have a small wooden addition to house a flush toilet: the outer door would open outwards and have a lockable push bar handle: extra coat pegs would be installed.
- the entrance door to the Juniors' porch would be bricked up, two individual showers to be installed on a raised plinth and a small wooden addition built to house a flush toilet.
- the large stove would be removed from the classroom and the question of heating the building would be addressed.
- A look through the windows of the school house showed that wallpaper was peeling from the walls. The entire house would be re-decorated.

The work would be given to a local builder and supervised by a private firm of architects.

I drove home with the knowledge that all the work should be completed in time for us to move to Minstead on 1st September.

* * *

We lived in a large four-bedroomed house, built in light brick, that we had bought new in 1963: it was on the new Charlton Heights development on the Eastern edge of Wantage. It had full central heating and a wide attached garage. A high brick wall gave the large rear garden privacy from the road. I had developed a very productive vegetable and fruit plot: a sandpit, a large steel framed swing and tubular steel frame slide edged the large lawn that provided ample space for the children to play and ride tricycle and bicycle.

* * *

Half term came: I had to put my students in for their external exams and was busy discharging my duties as Chief Examiner in Rural Studies for a regional examination board.

I relinquished my responsibilities on the area Rural Studies advisory panel and as Chair of the Berkshire Science exam panel.

Sadly I said farewell as Hon. Sec. of the Berkshire Rural Studies Association for Teachers, and as Chairman of the North Berkshire Bee Keepers Association.

* * *

August and we obtained a nine-week old male Tabby kitten, to be neutered; when introduced into our lounge, the eyes nearly "popped out" of our large Rhodesian Ridgeback dog Buster who was restrained by Gill – he had spent his life chasing cats! We had brought Buster back to England when we left Rhodesia in 1960.

Two plants to take from the garden – a cultivated Blackberry, "Himalayan Giant" with large fruits, and a double yellow highly scented climbing rose, "Maigold"! These would be pruned severely and planted in black sacks of soil.

Oh! Yes! The house: we managed to sell it privately to a Lieutenant-Colonel in the Royal Engineers who had distinguished himself as a "bomb disposal" expert in Northern Ireland – he thought that he had used up "all his nine lives"!

The bees. I reduced the number of stocks in my two out apiaries, at Rowstock under Harwell Down and in my doctor's orchard in Wantage by selling some and giving some to ex-pupils. I would take 8 stocks plus all my spare hives and equipment to Minstead.

Early on a Sunday morning mid-August Roger Humphries arrived with a large Ford van – an ex-beekeeping pupil he was now a partner in his father's painting and decorating firm. Loading up the hives of live bees and all the equipment we drove steadily to Minstead with no jolts or sudden braking!

We placed the bee hives on bearers at the top of the school field, opened the hive entrances and retired swiftly! Equipment we stowed in the wooden garage on the yard.

Builders "bits" everywhere: would they be finished by 1st September?

CHAPTER 3

THE MOVE

The large pantechnican arrived on 1st September, "all our worldly goods" were loaded and finally, with the large tailboard down, the sections of my Hall's cedarwood garden shed were lashed on. Away it went.

The MG Magnette was loaded with three young children, a large dog and a kitten in a basket. Farewells said, waved off by our neighbours, we drove out of Elm Road en route for our new life in the New Forest.

We arrived at Minstead school well before the pantechnican. On the yard, by the garage, was our maroon coloured Mini saloon: the previous Sunday my father-in-law had accompanied me down with it, as Gillian had failed her driving test in Newbury two weeks earlier.

Whilst the family enjoyed the picnic given to us by our Elm Road neighbours, then played on the lawn, I wandered around the school and the house. Little progress seemed to have been made: the extensions were still being made and most of the school and the house still had to be decorated!

During the afternoon our furniture and goods were offloaded and placed in the correct rooms: on the lawn, by the yew tree, lay the sections of my garden shed and the dismantled swing and slide.

We would obviously camp out in the house that night!

Up the stairs from the front door hallway were two narrow bedrooms over the school dining room, one facing the front lawn, the other the yard. A passage from the upstairs landing

Family August 1967

led to a medium-size bedroom, over the school kitchen – facing on to the yard – and a large master bedroom that looked on to the front lawn.

Downstairs, a passage from the hall led through a front-facing large lounge to a small, front facing dining room, thence to a narrow kitchen facing on to the road. The dining room and kitchen comprised the single storey addition that had been built on to the house.

A bathroom? Part of the kitchen, sectioned off by a 6ft high wooden screen with door was the "bathroom" in which was squeezed a narrow roll-top bath, a wash basin and a wall-mounted electric water heater: a small hopper window faced the road.

All the bedrooms and the lounge had fireplaces. The kitchen had a wall unit, a work surface with cupboard storage below: an elderly 3 plate electric stove, a deep porcelain sink by the large window completed the kitchen facilities. All waste water from the kitchen was piped under ground to the cess pit.

In this house our family would have to live: during the coming weeks Gillian created our home in spite of workmen hanging wallpaper and applying paint.

* * *

A quick scan of the field – the roofs of two beehives had been knocked off. Close inspection showed that commoners' cows had forced their way through the roadside hedge and had grazed the field, leaving plenty of evidence behind! With the help of two workmen the gap in the hedge was plugged with odd bits of timber and wire. My first encounter with local livestock that roamed around the village!

* * *

Minstead Centre (1970)

Elm Road House

The next day we drove into Lyndhurst to visit the C. of E. Primary School opposite the church. Lyndhurst had changed during the year since I did the Forestry Commission course; cattle grids close to the village prevented livestock from walking through the village and there was now a one-way street system in operation – traffic flowed in one direction only.

We were welcomed by the elderly Headmistress: Sandy would catch the circular route school bus at 8:15am at the Trusty Servant stop in Minstead and would return there by 3:30pm in the afternoon.

Jane, 18 months old and John aged four would be at home: we would have to find a part-time playgroup for John in due course.

A meeting at The Castle, Winchester, to discuss the new Studies Centre, chaired by Miss Zeta Ferguson, chief education officer for Primary education, Mr Ralph Dulson the county primary schools advisor and senior administrative officer Mr Leslie Crowfoot. It had been decided that the centre would be called "Minstead Rural Studies Centre" and that as the secondary schools had exclusive use of the Calshot Spit Centre, they would not be able to use the Minstead Centre – it would be Primary schools only! I had lost my older, secondary school element!

* * *

Future staffing discussed: as finances were tight, a part time secretary now, other staff to start in the New Year by which time all builders work should have been completed – advice – "advertise widely".

In the meantime sell my Centre and ideas to the county schools and the new Teachers' Centres: I would be paid the official mileage rate on top of my head teacher salary.

A pub lunch afterwards with Ralph Dulson. He had been head of a school in London before being appointed Primary

Schools Advisor for Hampshire: visiting the Forest with his school groups he had noted the Minstead school in its delightful location.

The large gypsy encampment in Shave Green, well-established before the war, had many children who attended Minstead school. By 1965 the authorities had decided that all the gypsies would be cleared from Shave Green in the Forest: they would all be resettled in houses in the Waterside parishes. By Spring 1966 this had taken place with the result that school numbers at Minstead School had fallen by a half to eighteen children, infants and juniors – not really viable.

Ralph had the job of inspecting the school and recommended the inevitable closure of the school in July 1966. He had the idea of a studies centre there and eventually sold the idea to Mrs Ferguson!

* * *

The village had lost its school: there was much resentment.

There was much speculation in the village about what was going to happen at the old school. Among the ideas – I was going to teach the Commoners how to farm and look after their animals – I was going to set up a "nature" or nudist camp!

One evening in late September I thought it wise to walk up to the village and make myself known at the Trusty Servant pub. The resident publican had been a police station sergeant in Wednesbury, Staffordshire and kept his truncheon hanging up behind the bar.

He pulled my pint of beer, gave me the change, then leaning on the bar with a grin on his face asked "What are you going to do down there then?" So I explained my overall ideas for visiting school children from around the county "Oh! That's not what they have thought in the village!"

A week later, a persistant sore throat caused me to consult the doctor, Dr Danby who held a teatime surgery in the Village

Hall. After examination and writing a prescription he asked me the inevitable question "What was I going to do down at the school?" So, I explained my ideas. He sat back, smiled, and said "So you are a Naturalist, not a Naturist!"

* * *

Tuesday morning of the Autumn half-term saw me driving the family to Newbury in our maroon Mini: Gill was booked to have an hour-long revisory lesson with her old driving school followed by a re-sit of the driving test around the Newbury circuit in the driving school's saloon: she had spent two hours the previous Sunday afternoon manoeuvering the Mini around my obstacle course on the school yard!

The children and I spent the next two hours shopping and driving around Newbury. Returning to the rendezvous we found Gill with a large grin on her face and clutching some important documents: she had passed her re-sit and proceeded to drive us back to Minstead in her maroon Mini – nicknamed "Gillie's Gig"!

* * *

The shop by the village green, owned by Mrs Bowden, was the source of a wide variety of groceries, confectionary and newspapers. In a glass-fronted kiosk was the Post Office with postmistress Mrs Robinson: until 1966 she had run it at her house, Hengerford Cottage, on Running Hill Road but then it was transferred to the shop on the Village Green.

On the corner of Seamans Lane and Running Hill Road was another shop: with a large front window it was part of the house there and run by the Hitchcock family. It sold a variety of groceries and confectionary: by the roadside it had a single petrol pump.

We did most of our shopping in Lyndhurst. There were two branches of the International Stores, one by the T-junction at the top of the High Street, the other next to Barclays Bank opposite the garage.

Pink and Stretch, opposite the T-junction, was a large shop, extending backwards up a slope to a raised section of shop: from there a door led to workshops. The shop sold a wide variety of hardware, garden tools and sundries, carpentry and D.I.Y tools: planed timber would be cut to size and glass, cut to size, could be ordered: paraffin was dispensed into your container.

In the Lyndhurst High Street was a wide variety of shops: several butchers and greengrocers, a fishmonger, a branch of Elliots selling shoes and men's clothing, a bespoke leather goods shop, and a curio shop selling soft toys. There were dress shops, ladies' hair-dressers, 2 barbers, 2 chemists, antique shops, a bakers and inns. The Post Office was just below the Crown Hotel. There were 3 banks, Barclays, Lloyds and Midland, a large bookshop, solicitors' offices and architects' offices. In the adjoining public car park a branch of the H.C.C. library was at one end of the Community Centre.

The New Forest Garage, off the bottom of the High Street sold new and used B.M.C. cars – Austin, Morris, MG, Riley, Wolseley – a large workshop did servicing and repair work. The forecourt adjoining the road had a variety of petrol pump. We could fill up the near-empty petrol tank of our Mini for a "Fiver".

Lyndhurst High Street was the natural shopping centre and focal point for this central region of the New Forest. Indeed, Lyndhurst was "The Capital of the New Forest!"

* * *

Slow progress was being made by the builder. A tall painter/decorator from Totton was busy working in the house lounge: he had stripped off the old wallpaper and was cleaning the plaster in the walls prior to hanging the new wallpaper: he took a pen, then printed and signed his name together with the date at shoulder height on the wall. They always did this so that in years to come it would be known who had papered the wall.

* * *

I held interviews then appointed Mrs Mona Spikins from Ashurst as my part-time Secretary, to start after half-term working five mornings a week. Her husband was a Merchant Navy Captain on the banana boat run: they had a schoolgirl daughter.

* * *

Head Forester John Middleton of Northerwood House, drove me through the Highland Water Inclosure pointing out the different forestry operations going on there and helping my identification of the many tree species there. I was given permission to walk through there with my Ridgeback dog Buster.

We walked the Open Forest within a three mile radius of the school recording in my field note-book items and places of interest.

CHAPTER 4

GETTING TO KNOW THE VILLAGE

We soon got to know the area around the Village Green – this seemed to be the nodal point of the village.

On the right of the road going up to the church were a pair of semi-detached cottages known as Crofton Cottages. These had been acquired by NFDC from Minstead Estate in 1954 and converted into cottages prior to the Council taking possession.

The property had been known as "The New Room" and was originally erected for the purposes of "technical education".

The only dwelling between these and the church was a recently built white painted house lying well back from the road – "Whitethorn" was owned by Mr and Mrs Jack Collins.

* * *

The three attached COMPTON COTTAGES, set well back from the road, had been built by NFDC in 1952. The land had been purchased by NFCD from Minstead Estate in 1937 as an alternative to a "clearance order" being made upon the two cottages that stood on the lane: they had been associated with the forge.

The estate smithy/forge that stood at the roadside had been partially destroyed accidentally by an army tank during the Second World War!

Compton Cottages 1968

Dunbridge Cottage 1968

Opposite the Smithy, nestling on the roadside below "Ye Olde Trusty Servant" inn had once been the Wheelwright's Cottage, Wisteria Cottage, the two crafts linked in the making of wheels for wagons. Now, in 1967, close to the road was a pair of semi-detached cottages, known as Wisteria Cottages.

* * *

The large field behind Compton Cottages and stretching behind the Old Rectory was ancient GLEBE land associated with the Church. In "1967 or thereabouts" a parcel of this Glebe land was bought by NFDC from the Parish. Together with a small piece of land purchased from Minstead Estate, these two parcels of land formed the site on which CONGLETON CLOSE was to be built.

* * *

On the corner of the narrow lane leading to London Minstead, and nearly opposite the end of Compton Cottages was Dunbridge Cottage, a tile-roofed property lived in by Mrs Merriman. A little further along the narrow lane a field gateway led to a modern 3 bedroomed house built in the field: Minstead Manor Farm Cottage was home to the Eldridge family – he was the cowman at Manor Farm, the farm on the road to the Watersplash and the school that was owned by Mrs Strange.

* * *

The Old Rectory, a dominant feature on the East side of the Village Green, has a red-brick two storey stable block backing on to the roadway. As the Rectory with the adjoining Glebe land field, it had housed three successive Rectors who had been members of the Compton family from 1842 to 1931 – a

Wisteria Cottage 1968

Congleton Close 1975

continuous span of 89 years. The present rector, Revd. Rham lives in Glebe Cottage on the main road towards Lyndhurst.

* * *

The large red-brick house, The Old Cottage, was built by the Compton Manor Estate by 1728: in 1921 it was the official home of the AGENT of the Compton's Manor Estate.

* * *

In early Autumn came news that shocked Minstead: Lord Congleton had been killed in a car accident on the notoriously busy A34 Winchester By-pass. A batchelor, he had been very active in village life. The "seat" of the Congletons was Minstead Lodge, an imposing grey-stone mansion on a hill top of London Minstead looking down over their fields and paddocks towards Football Green. His mother, the Dowager Duchess had divided her time between Minstead and their estate in Scotland that included a West coast island.

The house had an extensive, typical Victorian brick-walled front and vegetable garden that had several lean-to green houses.

The estate owned properties in London Minstead including Home Farm in which resided their ancillary staff.

The house opposite to our ccntre is called "The Splash"; it was built on orchard land in the 1920s for a Colonel Elliot. Mr George Northcroft C.B.E. now owns it and lives there with his sister: he is chair of the Parish Council and is our County Councillor.

At the top of Fleetwater Hill is the red-brick Fleetwater Cottage occupied by Miss Pultenay who, with her mother, bought it in 1955. Originally belonging to the Manor Estate it was their "gamekeepers cottage".

Opposite is the modern light-brick house built in 1957 on land that had been the garden plot for the gamekeepers's cottage opposite. It is owned by an architect Mr Geoffrey Tear who resides there with his family.

Fleetwater House, the large modern red-brick house was built around 1935: a staff house was built near the entrance gates. The present owner/occupier is Mrs Phelps. During the 1939-45 war it hosted an evacuated private school.

* * *

Fleetwater Farm is occupied and farmed by the Penny family: buildings include the red brick farmhouse, built 1879-81, and large brick built barn. There are pasture fields adjoining the farm and also up the lane leading towards Furzey House. The herd of milking dairy cows slowly walked past the Centre each day on their way to and from the pasture fields up Furzey Lane.

* * *

Next to Fleetwater Farm is the Off-Licence Cottage, built of brick, with thatched roof. It has a licence to sell alcohol (ales) to passers-by to be consumed "off the premises". Adjoining the cottage is some land and a large yard with out-buildings. The cottage is occupied by Mr Jack Whitehorn and family: he was caretaker at the school and is the "church grave-digger." On the opposite side of the road from the cottage there are brick pig-stys on the wide road verge.

* * *

EDWARDIAN WHEELWRIGHT

Mr. Charles Pavey was an Estate Carpenter and Wheelwright at Odstock Nr. Salisbury before moving to Wisteria Cottage, Minstead as Estate Carpenter for Squire Compton at Minstead Manor but as work was getting slack on the Estate he started up on his own with his son Charles and eventually was a builder and employed his son and six men on occasions when extra busy.

He bought trees and a Mr. Paintor would cut them down and saw them into planks which were stacked on his yard to dry out for his use as carpenter and wheelwright.

He had a big tool and paintshop with a bandsaw and circular saw run by an engine. He also had a man from Lyndhurst called a Liner by trade to paint lines on carts, etc., and also the names of people.

Mr. Pavey built wagons, light carts and heavy carts, handcarts and wheelbarrows.

There weren't any cars in those days and he had a wagonette, two Victorias and a Landau which was used to drive people to Southampton to catch trains. He also let out these to people who could drive horses.

The children of Minstead used to have great fun when he made wheels for carts. He would take them across the road to Mr. Phillps the blacksmith across the road to bond the wheels with iron tyres and after it was finished the children brought potatoes and put them in the ashes to bake. They really enjoyed them and they looked rather dirty with black faces and hands by the time the potatoes were ready.

Mr. Pavey passed away in July 1913.

NB. This information is taken from a letter sent to the Author by Mr. Billy Iremonger from Sydney, Australia in 1979.

CHAPTER 5

CHRISTMAS IS COMING!

In the weeks between half-term and Christmas there were several tasks that dominated my mind: -

1. The furnishing of the centre so that it would be ready to accommodate school visitors.
2. Exploring the vicinity as regards its use by day visitors and by residential groups.
3. Making a decision on the composition of a Day Visit both in good and inclement weather.
4. Advertising the Centre and my ideas to schools throughout the County.

* * *

A meeting at the Castle revealed that during July back-room staff had estimated the furniture that would be needed for the Centre. There would be bunk beds to sleep 24 pupils with bed-side lockers for each child, wardrobes for clothes, whilst outdoor clothes and footwear would be kept in the cellars!

Tables and chairs for the classroom and the dining room had also been allowed for in the furnishings budget for this financial year.

I pointed out that the cellars had been filled in some time ago and that I would investigate the practicalities of the suggested furnishing.

* * *

At the Centre we measured the large classroom/dormitory-to-be: on graph paper. I drew a scale plan. Rectangular and square pieces of graph paper representing bunk beds and lockers were cut out and then the jig-saw puzzle began1

It became obvious that only twelve bunk beds could be squeezed in – no room for bedside lockers: clothes storage was a problem to be solved.

* * *

On the domestic side we received invaluable advice from our divisional School Meals Adviser, Miss Painter – who had been a high-ranking officer in the A.T.S. during the war. She re-organised the centre kitchen with new work-surfaces and storage spaces, a pair of new large, deep metal sinks with teak draining boards on either side, a large propane gas-powered cooking stove and a wall mounted electric hot-water heater.

* * *

One day she took Gillian to a secondary school in Winchester that had a boarding annex for some of their younger children so that she could meet the master-in-charge and his wife and discuss their modus operandi.

* * *

From somewhere she conjured up for the dining room a large metal framed electrically heated warming oven with interior metal shelving and an over-all chrome-steel top. Prepared hot food in B. S. tins could be kept warm until ready to be served at a meal time.

How it was manouvered into the dining-room I know not! It occupied the space between the door into the kitchen and the door into the house hallway and was waist high.

* * *

Furniture for the dining room was selected; four yellow formica-topped hexagonal tables each made up from two three-legged triangular halves that slotted together. Junior size light-oak finished stacking chairs with four adult chairs available completed the seating arrangements.

* * *

The dormitory would accommodate twenty children on bunk beds; two free-standing chest-of-drawers, one by each of the two large windows, would give twelve drawers to be shared. After allowing for classroom tables and chairs there was money to spare from the original generous budget; the construction of built-in furniture by the building firm would solve many problems.

* * *

Built-in units on either side of the big chimney breast in the dining room, and along the South and West facing wall of the classroom would be designed and constructed.

My secretary sat at her special desk in the corner of the dining room next to the School House with the telephone extension and new grey filing cabinet for her use.

* * *

We had learned about the Hampshire County Central Purchasing System. Officers at their offices on the outskirts of Winchester obtained significant discounts from suppliers and manufacturers by bulk ordering a wide range of goods. Each Hampshire establishment, whether police, fire, schools or colleges, etc. was issued with a catalogue of goods available: we each had our unique establishment number – our's was 9857.

Adjoining their offices was a vast warehouse where their large range of catalogued goods were stored. Outside was the fleet of pantechnican type lorries that delivered the goods on specified runs to all parts of the county.

On receipt of our requisition form, the goods would be costed, our account debited, and the goods delivered to us in the next scheduled "run" to our area, normally monthly.

A morning in early November was spent at The Castle discussing our furniture requirements with their "supplies officer": he would order direct from the suppliers and our furniture would be delivered direct to us by them during the week before Christmas.

* * *

The first route that I surveyed started at Robinsbush Cross Roads. There were several tall Silver Birch trees growing near the side of the main road just below the crossroads – on the wide grassy verge that was Manor Waste. High up, on side branches, were several "Witch's Brooms", clumps of small birch shoots growing from points on the branches and looking like large pin-cushions!

Some years earlier an air-borne spore of a particular fungus had entered a wound on the branch: there they had developed, eventually producing a growth hormone that caused the multi-twig growth; it also produced a dye that would eventually colour the branch-wood green.

* * *

On the right side of the lane was Robinsbush Farm: the remains of the farmhouse were end-on to the road fence. Next to it was a large dark- coloured roofed barn: beside was a metal 5-bar gate leading to the farm yard where there were several out-buildings

Pasture fields on either side, the lane went down a gentle slope with hedging plants on the left, a post and wire fence on the right. A bend to the right and steep slope led to a FORD where a small forest stream flowed over a concrete base that extended for several feet on either side.

A narrow path to the left led to a steel and concrete footbridge (over the little stream after it left the ford): the bridge had inbuilt metal handrails in the side,

* * *

Back on the lane, a very wide grassy verge, fence and pasture field on the left, a narrow verge, small trees and tall hedge on the right, a walk up the slope to a road junction.

To the left a road led to the buildings of Acres Down Farm some distance away.

In front a Forest roadway disappeared into a holly holm, up a steep slope to emerge on to the top of Acres Down. Following the near level track-way along the top of the Down it was possible to look over the heath towards Southampton where the red and black funnels of the giant Cunard liner, Queen Mary, stood out above the docklands area.

Back to the junction. The forest road continued, with the hillside of Acres Down on the left and an Inclosure fence on the right until it left the open forest woodland to enter Highland Water Inclosure through a Forestry Commission gateway.

Near the road junction the Inclosure fence did a right-angle turn to turn roughly in the direction of Stoney Cross.

* * *

A driveway from the junction led to ACRES DOWN HOUSE that faced the Inclosure: there were several mature deciduous trees on the wide piece of land between the house and Inclosure. Several bird-boxes had been attached about 10ft up the oak trunks.

Acres Down House and the two adjoining small properties are owned by Mr S.Warwick Warwick-Haller, a member of the legal profession, and his wife also is the County Girl Guides Commissioner for Hampshire. The house was built in 1922 on a 2 acre site bought from Minstead Manor Estate. It was built for Major Darling and came in sections from Boulton and Paul Ltd in Norwich – a wooden house erected on a brick foundation and given a thatch roof: it was then called "Aldermoor". During the 1940s the thatch was replaced by a tile roof: since then additions have been built on the West End, the walls pebble-dashed and a double garage built.

The site is completely surrounded by Minstead Manor Waste land. Mr Warwick-Haller showed me round his garden of about one-and-three quarter acres in which he has personally planted, in recent years, over 30 different species of Conifers, and 70 different other trees and shrubs. He does not employ a gardener and is justifiably proud of his collection.

* * *

I returned to the Inclosure fence that ran parallel to the forest roadway: the fence was a good example of the traditional fence-

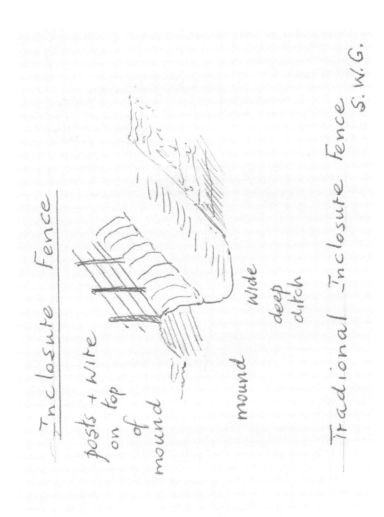

Inclosure Fence

ditch-and-bank with post and wire fence on top of the bank. Growing behind the fence were some tall, mature trees – several Scots Pines well furnished with immature cones; – the wide grassy verge on which I walked strewn with old cones – there was also a Sessile Oak, relatively rare with acorns growing directly from the twig, whereas the common Pedunculate Oak has acorns growing on stalks.

* * *

On the other side of the road was a piece of hard-standing ground where people parked their cars; silver birch, holly and crab apple trees grew nearby.

To sum up – this area that I had walked from Robinsbush Crossroads was full of interest.

* * *

Advertising the existence of the Centre had begun: mention of it had been made at a local headteachers' meeting: this led to the Headmaster of a large Totton junior school inviting me to have morning coffee with him at the school. It soon became apparent that the Heads thought I was a recently retired Military Man who had been drafted in to run the Centre, in the same way that a Navy Man, Wingate, had been appointed to set up the Calshot Spit Centre! The atmosphere changed when I explained my education experience and gave a rough idea of what schools would do at the Centre. Over the years Rees and I became firm friends.

* * *

The South-West Division stretched along the coast to the outskirts of Bournemouth and included Highcliffe and

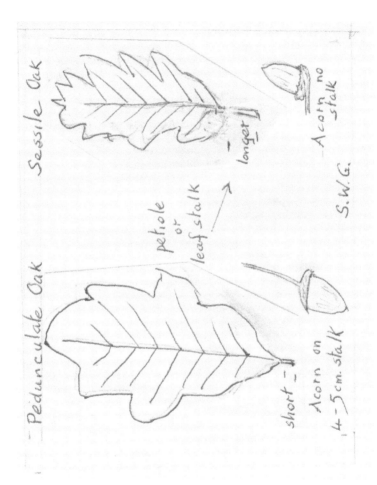

Oak leaves and acorns

Christchurch. Highcliffe had many new housing developments: the head of the large junior school, Mr Bob Chacksfield, was very proud of the standards in his school, especially of their school choir who regularly won area competitions under the baton of Miss Dennis, a teacher.

Christchurch was also expanding as a desirable housing area close to Bournemouth. Somerford was a large self-contained residential estate. Over coffee, Jack, the head of the large junior school, told me of the estate, bounded by the old A35 main road on one side and the new by-pass on the other. Most of his pupils had never been off the estate during their life-time there! A coach trip to Minstead in the Forest would be life-changing experience for them! Yes! His school would visit us!

Teachers' Centres were in their infancy. There would be one in each division or area: situated in a room or an annex of an existing educational establishment, and staffed by a teacher on secondment, they would provide a place for teachers to enjoy meetings and courses, mainly in out-of-school hours.

I visited many of them to give tea-time talks about the Centre. Journeys were made northwards up the Test Valley to the old market town of Andover now rapidly expanding with London overspill and to the other old market town of Basingstoke also expanding with London overspill.

Over the race-horse training Downs to Kingsclere near the Berkshire border where I discovered that at the top of the church tower was a windvane in the shape of a "Bed-Bug", placed there on the orders of a King of England to warn travellers not to stay there – he had suffered on his one-night stay! The headmaster of Kingsclere Junior School was, at week-ends, a top class football referee regularly taking Division One matches. Some years later the Football Association rewarded him with the Cup Final as his last match before retirement.

* * *

To the east of the county was Havant a rapidly expanding township swollen with Portsmouth overspill: further north was the market-town of Petersfield near the county border with Sussex.

Aldershot with nearby expanding Farnborough in the North-East corner of the county, close to the Surrey border shared a new Centre. Further north I went to a tea-time meeting at Hawley where a road-sign stated "London, 32 miles" – I looked at my car milometer, it read 65 miles to Minstead: I realised how huge was the county of Hampshire that now employed me!

* * *

End of term approached and it became obvious that the work of the builders in renovating and improving the Centre buildings would not be completed by Christmas. It would drag on well into the New Year – disappointment all round.

CHAPTER 6

SETTING UP THE CENTRE

Early in January 1968 I was assured by both the private architects and the building firm that all the improvement and refurbishment work in the Centre would be completed by the February half-term. At last a date to aim at – we would be able to start taking Day Visitors after the half-term break.

Staff had to be appointed and advertisements were placed locally. With the help of Miss Painter we interviewed and appointed our first cook Mrs Sybil Harrison of Broughton Road, Lyndhurst: she had been a school meals cook at Copythorne School during the war years.

As a cleaner for the Centre, initially for three hours per day we appointed Mrs Eldridge from Manor Farm Cottage, whose husband was cowman at Manor Farm.

To maintain the grounds and the garden I appointed a Minstead man to work one day per week, normally Friday. Mr Robinson lived in London Minstead and had been chauffeur at the Congleton estate. The estate had now started to sell off properties in London Minstead.

In spite of the inconvenience of the School House in which we lived, Gillian did a marvellous job in providing a family home for three children, the eldest just 7 years old, a large Ridgeback dog, Sammy the Tabby cat, and me!

Opposite our back kitchen door four steep steps led up to

a small brick building with wood-lined roof and 3 doors, 1 at the front, 1 at the side, one at the back. It had obviously been a "privy", toilet, for the house in its early days. The largest section, facing our back door, I shelved for Gill to use as her vegetable store.

Every Saturday morning a man came to our back door to see what fruit and vegetables we would like to buy for our family. It was Mr Jim Coffin who lived in a house by the side of Football Green: it faced Minstead Cricket Club ground and Jim had been a keen, leading member of the club for many years.

On the upper part of the grassy school field was a saucer-shape depression some 12 feet in diameter: every time there was heavy rain the saucer filled with water, about 8 inches deep in the middle. My hives of bees were on the dry, higher, corner of the field adjacent to the road-side hedge. Negotiations with the head of the Schools Grounds Dept. in Winchester, led to the squad of men arriving in their large green van to deal with this problem. They laid an underground pipe system that discharged the rainwater half-way down the big bank at the side of the yard. We would be able to use the whole field whatever the weather.

* * *

The roadside post box, near Skymers drive, on the higher land of the Robinsbush to Stoney Cross road was of great interest. The red facia bore the insignia "V.R", i.e. of Victorian Vintage!

Crossing the road we are still on Minstead Manor Waste land with some small Scots Pine trees and heathplants. There are several deep pits where the stones and gravels occurring there were excavated for road making in times gone by.

There is also the remains of a Honey Bee site, an approximately 12 feet square where the earth had been dug out to a two foot depth and been used to build an earth wall around the site. Beekeepers would have brought straw skeps of bees there to harvest the Heather Honey in August: the earthen walls would give the skeps a degree of protection from bad weather.

* * *

Following a narrow path down hill through the heathplants we came to the valley bottom – here, surrounded by willow trees is a wide shallow Ford across a small forest stream. The stream, like most forest streams, is born in a bog – this extensive bog has a maximum depth of over 5 feet. This ford is named Ringwood Ford Bottom.

Ascending the slope on the other side we leave Manor Waste land and go on to Crown land and follow the Inclosure fence line through a Holly Holm to the top of the valley where the ground levels out. A gateway leads into the Inclosure plantations.

Nearby, on slightly higher land , Hart Hill, is an Ordnance Survey triangulation point. The tall white stone Trig Point has information plaques on the side and a 3 prong brass grooving where the theodolytes would be fixed when Triangulation for map making was undertaken.

* * *

Westwards from this Trig. Point our track went along the edge of an old mixed broadleaf woodland, Stonard Wood, – elderly oaks and beeches in varying states of health and decrepidation – with an evergreen "understorey" of holly and yew.

Between our track and the Inclosure fence is a wide strip, at least 30/40 yards wide, of short, heath vegetation: this is a "Fire-Break" strip, kept mown short, to prevent fire from spreading from the open forest into the plantation in the Inclosure.

* * *

Trig. point

Gravel pit and Buster

At the Western end of the old woodland, facing the distant A31 road are several shorter oak trees. The end one is partly hollow with a hole, about 4" diameter, in the trunk about 10ft above ground level. On a mild day. honey bees can be seen flying in and out of the hole. No doubt a swarm from an apiary that has established itself permanently in the hollow trunk!

* * *

Back to our trackway. The whole width of the firebreak land was occupied by a Pony Round-up and Branding Station utilizing the Inclosure fence as one side with an arrangement of posts, and rails giving small corrals, sorting gates and a one animal size branding pen. Built and maintained by the Agister and the area Commoners the station was used for the periodic "round-up" of all ponies in the area. Herding the ponies along the firebreak land from the West, the ponies were moved into a large funnel formed by the Inclosure fence and a post and rail fence: the funnel ended in a corral from which ponies could be sorted.

On the ground were the remains of wood fires used to heat the Branding Irons: some brand marks had been singed into posts and rails.

From here our trackway went down hill, across a shallow ford, then climbed up a hill, Mogslade Hill, to disappear in the direction of Ringwood. One may surmise that this trackway running Westwards from Ringwood Ford Bottom was an ancient "trackway route" from Minstead to Ringwood.

* * *

Near the Round-up station a gateway led into Puckpits Inclosure, of historic origin and now incorporated into the large Highland Water Inclosure. A narrow path led under a line of tall conifer trees, down a steep slope to meet a broad track that connected plantations.

At the side of this track stood "Barney's Beech", a very old pollarded tree that had ten trunks growing out from its major trunk about 8 feet above ground level. Although well furnished with leaves the presence of bracket fungi on the main trunk indicated signs of decay.

In the 17th Century a forest ruling forbade the pollarding of oak and beech trees; good straight trunks were needed for future naval timber. Commoners had practised pollarding – cutting off the many shoots that could be used to produce foliar feed for their animals.

Barney's Beech, pollarded before this ruling, must be at least 300 years old. Imagine the dress of all the people who had walked under the tree in that time!

* * *

This route that I had walked from the Victorian Post box, via Ringwood Ford Bottom, the Pony Round-up Station and Barney's Beech was full of interest to people of all ages.

* * *

Several days a week I visited schools that had booked to visit the Centre for a day during the second half of the term, to meet the Heads and Staff, outline the arrangements and meet the children.

* * *

At week-ends I was still exploring forest areas. Starting near the bee Tree, by the Pony Round-up Station, a narrow path descended steeply through the heathland to a small stream –

Barney's Beech

LONG BROOK, that originated in a heathland bog, Withybed Bottom. Over the stream a bridge had been constructed in memory of an Admiral who had died whilst hunting in the forest: it was known as "Admiral's Passage".

A small pool of varying depth had been formed under and on either side of the bridge as the stream trickled its way in the direction of Ringwood. Patient watching revealed small fish and newts in the pool: they had protection from the variety of aquatic plants in the stream.

From the bridge, our narrow track ascended out of the valley to a fairly level area of heathland: here, at right-angles to our path, was a broad, grassy forest road. On the north side of this road were two separate large pools that had been formed by past gravel extractions.

The first pool, with an irregular shaped shoreline had a good variety of both terrestrial and aquatic plants: there was some aquatic animal life.

The second, larger pool had a notice by it – "Southampton Model Boat Club". Members used to sail a wide variety of engine and also sail powered boats. Fascinating to watch them, especially at weekends. A little further up the roadway the Forestry Commission had created a car park area for them that was accessed by a stony roadway from the Minstead to Stoney Cross road.

* * *

At long last the builders had completed their work and had cleared away all their equipment!

The three rooms of the Centre were spick and span, the windows had been cleaned and deliveries of dry foods had arrived and been stored in the kitchen pantry.

All was ready for our first day visitors after half-term!

CHAPTER 7

THE CENTRE OPENS

On the Tuesday after half-term our first school arrived for a day visit. We were in business!

The top class of WEST TYTHERLEY C. OF E. PRIMARY SCHOOL with their teacher and Head Master arrived in their hired coach at about 10.00am. The coach backed up near to the Centre gates. A group at a time the children were sent up the yard to the toilets, then back on to the coach, where I joined them.

We took the coach over the ford, past Fleetwater Farm and the Old Off-Licence to Robinsbush Cross Roads. It backed down the road to be level with the big Silver Birch trees.

Off we got, examined the deeply fissured silvery trunk and looked up to discover Witch's Brooms. Then a slow wander down the lane past Robinsbush Farm looking at the poultry, sheep and cows in the fields.

We examined the ford, walked over the little bridge, up the lane and followed it to level with Acres Down car park. The Inclosure Fence – would it be easy to get through? Standing in the ditch, the bank and fence would be too high for us and for cattle and ponies. Never go up to a pony – it could kick!

* * *

The giant Scots Pine had some orangy patches of bark on their trunks: leaves were like needles and the branches had greenish cones on them. On the ground by our feet were old pine needles, and old brown pine cones some of which still had small winged seeds in them. Many things to be put in our collecting bags.

* * *

By the roadside were large gorse bushes with their yellow flowers: no leaves, but green "spines" instead – would they protect the bush? I cut off a small shoot with flowers on to be taken back to their school.

A steady stroll back to the coach at Robinsbush Cross Roads, then back to the Centre.

Off the coach, wait by the wall: group at a time to the toilets, wash hands in the porch wash basins and sit at a table in the classroom. Staff use the toilet, newly built, by the porch entrance door.

Ready for lunch. A warm, home-made type of Cornish Pasty (Mrs Harrison's speciality), salad sandwiches and a shortbread biscuit – all prepared in the Centre kitchen and served by Mrs Harrison, Gillian and her cleaner, Mrs Eldridge. A glass of water or diluted Robinson's Orange Squash to drink. "Seconds" were shared out.

* * *

Then outside to wash hands and some supervised playtime on the yard whilst the plates and glasses were taken to the kitchen and tables wiped down.

Back in the classroom they gathered around in a semi-circle, the tables having been moved to the back of the room. From under a cloth I brought out a pair of Fallow Deer Feet. A foot has twin toes with a small gap between them; they are dark and shiny on the top. When walking on soft ground the toes leave a distinct footprint: this is called a "slot" and by following the trail of "slots" we can see where the deer has gone. I produced two small metal trays of soft clay soil in which I had made "slots" with a foot. The two deer feet and two trays of slots were passed around for close inspection.

* * *

I showed a large picture of Fallow deer: the male, called a "buck" had a pair of "antlers" on his head; the females, called "does" had no antlers.

Then, from under a sheet I produced a pair of Fallow "antlers" that had belonged to a 7 or 8 year old buck. Every Spring the antlers were "shed" – dropped off the head on to the ground! During the summer months a new pair of antlers grew from two "buds" on the Buck's Head: as they grow these soft bony antlers are covered in a soft furry skin called "velvet" that protects and nourishes them.

By early Autumn the new antlers have finished growing, the bone hardens and the buck starts "fraying" his new antlers by rubbing them against branches and tree trunks to get rid of the drying velvet and to harden the bone so that the new antlers will be ready for fighting with when the mating or "rutting" season start. Each year the buck grows a slightly larger pair of antlers. The two antlers were passed around for inspection.

* * *

Time was up. The Headteacher thanked us. Mrs Harrison had come in through the dividing door, there were "3 cheers" and our visitors filed out to go to the toilet, then back on their coach by 2pm allowing them time to get back to West Tytherley in time for their minibuses at school.

Our first Day Visitors! We had all enjoyed it.

* * *

On the next two mornings as the school coaches drove down the lane to us our elderly farming neighbour strode into the lane, stopped them, and told the driver that they had no right to use the lane! They continued down to us. It was pointed out to the farmer by Hampshire that the coaches had a legal Right of Access. The Education Office had decided, for the time being, to subsidise schools by paying the cost of their coaches when visiting the Centre.

For the remainder of the term we had 3 or 4 day visitors per week, but none in the last week of term. On the "spare" days I visited the schools who had booked to come into residence in the Summer Term.

* * *

Having walked more of the local area I had now decided on activities for the summer visitors. I had an appointment with the Deputy Surveyor in Queen's House, Mr Arthur Cadman, told him of my plans and the sites that I would like to use in the Forest. Could I have permission to use these sites. He agreed that we would have sole use of the sites. He told me of the book that he had written that was being published – title "Dawn, Dusk and Deer". He would later autograph a copy for me.

* * *

For many years it had been my belief that the majority of children had little or no contact with animals, especially farm animals: this was reinforced as I drove around Hampshire and saw the high density housing estates where a lot of our future visitors resided.

I decided that the Centre would keep a variety of small animals that would provide the contact for both residential and day visitors. The County grounds squad divided up the field into the "runs" that I had specified using oak posts and 6 ft wire netting one and a half inch gauge, the netting sunk into the ground 6 inches as a fox-proof measure.

On the edge of the field, from the toilet block end round to by the kitchen, they made a 2ft wide hardcore/gravel pathway from which there was access to each run via an oak-posted 2ft wide 5ft high wire net gate secured by "bolts" and "hasps and staples".

Visiting children on the path would be able to see the animals through the wire netting fence. In the runs we would keep a variety of ducks, geese and poultry. A commercially manufactured poultry house in each run would give secure night-time quarters; these houses raised up 6 inches above ground level to deter rats from nesting underneath them.

* * *

On the front lawn I would have several moveable arks to house Rabbits and Guinea Pigs. No commercial arks were suitable for my purpose, so many hours were spent in the lean-to-shed at week-ends and in the Easter Holiday working on a woodwork bench, that I had scrounged from a secondary school, constructing arks to my own design with wood from the embryo Totton Timber Co. by the railway sidings in Totton.

By late in the Easter holiday, having visited both professional and amateur animal breeders, I had selected and bought good specimens of the animals that I wanted. Foods would be stored in moisture proof bins in the lean-to shed and the food weighed out accurately on a "single-lever balance" from a science equipment supplier!

All the animals had to have names – most important to children – so my family had a good time choosing names.

So in residence we had – Percy the Rhode Island Red Cock with his three Light Sussex hens, – Dandy the Bantam Cock

Dandy the Bantam Cock

Nod the Muscovy Drake

with three Bantam Hens – Nod and Nina the pair of Muscovy ducks – Simon the Silkie cock with his 3 hens.

In five arks on the front lawn we had smooth-haired Guinea Pigs, Rough-haired Guinea Pigs and 3 buck rabbits – Dusty the Netherland Dwarf, Maori the New Zealand White, Elgar the Old English.

So who looked after them? At week-ends the old school caretaker, Jack Whitehorn, took the job of feeding morning and tea-time, and Friday tea-time. I got the funding to appoint a part-time odd-job man, 9.00am to 1.00pm, Monday to Friday. So the livestock aspect of the Centre was up and running by the end of the Easter holidays.

To equip the laboratory/classroom I took delivery of 2 glass and metal aquaria (18" x 12" x 12inch), and one of 24 x 12 x 12 inch size that I would use as Vivaria.

From a national supplier I bought a double-glazed Bee Observation Hive, with detachable ply-wood covers for the windows. Installed by the front window nearer the dormitory, the bees would walk through a tube, through a hole in the bottom of the window frame, to an alighting board on the external window sill. I would stock it with a Queen and Workers on 2 deep and 1 shallow frame from my bee hives. Two bottle feeders on the top allowed the giving of water and of sugar syrup.

The 2 vivaria and 1 cold water aquarium were on the wall benching further along the South wall, whilst on the benching by the West wall was a heated and aerated aquarium that would have Tropical Fish, and an electrically heated Observation Egg Incubator – with a clear plastic detachable dome roof that had a felt cover that could be placed over it. The incubator would hold 30 Fowl size eggs.

I intended that this room would be a place full of interest for both my Residential visitors and future Day visitors.

* * *

For wet weather protection we had ordered yellow P.V.C. macs and Sou-Westers for the residential children to wear: these were hung on the pegs in the Entrance Porch along with white P.V.C. macs for the teachers.

A second part-time cook had been found by Miss Painter and interviewed: we gave the lady from Totton a temporary appointment for the residential season.

We were "ready to go" after the Easter holiday!

CHAPTER 8

RESIDENTIAL

The first Monday morning of the Summer Term – 10.00am and a coach backed up to the Centre gates. Our first school party to stay in residence: twenty 11 year old boys from HURSLEY JUNIOR SCHOOL with a male teacher.

Each week of the Summer Term, except the last two, we entertained a party of either boys, or girls with their teacher. Patterns of activity evolved.

The Forest was our workshop – the place of discovery. We had no transport at the Centre so we walked everywhere, haversack on back containing picnic lunch. Sou-Westers were worn if showers were forecast – a frequent occurrence that summer! In fact, amongst the local gentry our parties became known as "THE LITTLE YELLOW PEOPLE – AREN'T THEY SWEET"!

ⵝ ⵝ ⵝ

Food: Breakfast, a cereal with milk, a cooked dish, served from the warming oven.

Picnic lunch, a variety of sandwiches and a screw-top plastic bottle of diluted Robinson's squash. On return to the Centre an apple and squash.

High tea at 5.00pm in the dining room with "home-cooking", hot main course and puddings, sometimes hot, sometimes cold. Water to drink.

A walk up the road to play rounders or football on the Manor Waste was followed by home made biscuits and milk.

* * *

On a Saturday morning in early May I drove to a farm at Arnewood near Sway with Sandra and John. The farm bred a variety of ducks and geese: we had come to buy a pair of goslings. The "pros and cons" of the different breeds were explained, then the breed most suited to our needs was recommended – "BUFF BACKS" – sexed, a pair of 6 week old goslings were carefully wrapped in sacking for us to take back to Minstead

* * *

The goslings were still covered mainly in "down" feathers: they must not be left out in rain, or they would get wet, have pneumonia and die!

We introduced them to their straw floored large poultry house and to their grassy run. A feed of "growers pellets", with water to drink from a large zinc metal water fount. Any rain and they would have to be ushered back into their house!

* * *

The goslings had to have names. No question about it – CHARLES and PETUNIA – the goose characters in the wonderfully written and illustrated American children's story books that John so enjoyed!

I spent Sunday at the workbench making a moveable, wire-netted shelter with plastic sheet roof into which the goslings could be driven if it rained: a hinged wire door would keep them in it.

This shelter was put in their run. From Monday onwards the staff would down tools and rush up to the field to usher the goslings into the shelter if rain arrived! This continued for several weeks until their first set of proper feathers had grown.

* * *

Mid-afternoon I would start taking two pairs of children at a time to feed and study the animals that they had chosen back at school. Water in a small zinc bucket from the stand pipe in the boys' urinal, rations of corn or pellets weighed out in the lean-to shed, taken up the path to the poultry run and put in the water fount and food trough there. Look in the nest box to see if any eggs were there: collect them then weigh them on the food balance and describe the colour and texture of the shell.

* * *

The arks of guinea pigs and rabbits had similar attention: fresh water in the stone bowl and pellets in the stone food bowl after the ark had been moved on to fresh grass that the animals could eat through the wire netting floor.

White-painted wood labels bearing Dymo-taped information about each animal(s) – name, breed – were attached to each ark and to the gate or wire fence of each poultry run.

In the future the livestock studies would be developed with duplicated animal outlines and I-Spy question sheets available for the children to use.

* * *

Thursday evening was parents' evening when they could visit the Centre and be shown round by their children. By half-term the visiting teachers advised me that "it was not such a good idea" as their task of showering and putting to bed excitable children was made more difficult.

Instead we decided to have an "OPEN AFTERNOON" on the Saturday before end of term when children took their families around the Centre: tea and biscuits were provided in the dining-room – fund raising for future special items.

Elgar in observation cage

Bed-time: when all were in bed and settled down I would always go in, have a few words and bid them "Good Night". The teacher stayed in the dormitory until all were asleep: then they came into the School House, upstairs to their front bedroom, over the dining room. I had wired up a listening device above the dormitory doorway with a speaker that could be switched on by the teacher in the bedroom. The teacher's accommodation was unsatisfactory: an alternative would have to be found in the next financial year.

* * *

Friday morning routines: "odd" numbers went to the Fleetwater Stream to observe and collect aquatic animal life whilst "evens" packed all their belongings in their cases to be taken out of the dormitory. Then the swap-over so that by mid-morning everyone had packed and had "dipped" the streams.

Back in the classroom, a drink of squash, then study and sketching of the aquatic specimens collected: Finally, the lesson of CONSERVATION – all these animals must be put back in the stream in the situation where they were found so that they can breed some more.

Lunch in the dining-room – two-course meal – similar to tea-time.

Farewells as they get aboard their coach that has backed-up during lunchtime and away they go by 2pm.

By 4.30 pm the Centre was "spick-and-span", ready to receive another group of visitors on Monday morning.

* * *

The need for a teaching assistant became obvious: I was working "round the clock"! Marie Chalk, an ex. Officer in the WRNS., who was a super-numary on the staff of Ringwood C. Junior School was "loaned" to the Centre for the second half of the 1968 Summer Term. She was officially seconded to the Centre from September onwards and was given a permanent appointment from April 1969 onwards.

* * *

The pattern for the AUTUMN TERM became:

- 6 weeks Residential in September/October with Parents' Saturday afternoon at the end of the sixth week.
- Day Visit parties after Half-term until end of November
- Visits to the Residential Schools and to Day Visit Schools for liaison and pre-teaching became a permanent feature of our programme.

* * *

This year, 1968, a General Election had been called for early May. I received a phone call from the Electoral Officer in Lyndhurst stating that they would require, as usual, the two schoolrooms as the local Polling Station!

I advised him that a school party would be in residence and that the big classroom was full of bunk beds: "cancel the school group and move the beds out" was the reply!

With the backing of the H.C.C. Education Dept., I rang the Electoral Officer to say they could not have the Centre as a Polling Station: "but where else can we go?" The Village Hall – oh! They had not thought of that!

Election Day came and although the Village Hall venue was well advertised old habits die hard.

I stood at the entrance gates at 9pm when two groups of people arrived to vote! "But, we always vote here" – "sorry, you have to go to the Village Hall to vote before 10pm"!

CHAPTER 9

NECESSARY ALTERATIONS AND ADDITIONS

During the Winter of 1968-69 a new single storey building, the Office Block, was erected on the yard, parallel to the Dining Room and set well back towards the field-bank: it had a flat roof and the external walls were clad with chestnut-coloured preservative coat vertical boarding.

Inside was a sizeable Teacher's bedroom with adjoining shower: a wash-basin/toilet unit and a rectangular office were on the other side of the external door.

In the entrance lobby we installed a Gestetner ink duplicating unit and small book shelf unit. The office had good built-in storage space and had two windows, one facing along the yard, the other looking down to the Centre kitchen.

A new wide flight of shallow steps, with handrail, led down to the Centre Kitchen. The working range in the kitchen was heated with Propane Gas: backing onto the shower block wall a shallow brick built storage unit was built to house the tall Propane Gas cylinders – inter-connected so that gas was taken from the second cylinder when the first was empty. When advised, the local contractor brought a new cylinder to replace the empty one.

I attached the dormitory listening device wire lead to the telephone wire lead from the main building to the office. The speaker/listening unit was now attached to the wall of the new teachers' bedroom, enabling them to hear what was going on in the dormitory.

* * *

The long, narrow front bedroom over the Centre dining room now reverted to family use: it was to be our bathroom. Standing just inside the doorway with Mr. G, the private architect, I scrutinised his plans – the loo to the left of the doorway with washbasin and bath backing on to the sloping ceiling about two-thirds of the way down the room.

"Yes, the toilet had to be there so that the effluent would go down to join the waste pipe from the front hallway toilet going to the cess pit in the front garden." "But, I shall be able to sit on the loo and wave to all my neighbours through the window!" "We could put toilet glazing in the window." "No, you cannot destroy the appearance of the frontage of this historic building!"

After much discussion, the wash basin pedestal would be put inside the door, the toilet and bath two-thirds of the way down the room, with a waste pipe running just below the ceiling level of the Dining Room to join the Hallway toilet waste. The entire length of the pipe, above curtain rail height, would be boxed in and painted to match the Dining Room décor!

The final five feet of our new bathroom would be partitioned off, with a door, to form a walk-in slatted shelved airing cupboard.

A similar partition in the rear bedroom provided much needed walk-in storage space. Work proceeded straight away.

* * *

The "bath room" end of our kitchen was removed to leave us with a long gallery kitchen with new fitted floor units, worktop and cupboards above stretching along one wall. Our new 12 cu. ft. chest freezer fitted along the wall from the little window whilst our Hoover Keymatic washing machine was plumbed in under the door-end draining board. A free-standing broom cupboard was just inside the door. At last Gillian had an up-to-date kitchen in which to cater for our family.

* * *

Central Heating was installed throughout the School House and Centre. A brick built boiler house was built over the passageway running to the side of the house. This housed a large automatic electronically controlled oil fuel burner, fed from a large oil tank in the garden next to the old loo block.

Two large tanks, water and over-flow, lifted through the enlarged roof manhole above the top of our stairs then maneuvered through the roof space to rest on bearers above the ceiling of our master bedroom; sometime music to our ears when in bed!

The 1969 Residential Session would start with much improved facilities.

* * *

However, Day Visits by whole classes posed problems on really wet days as our classroom/laboratory was quite small. Two alternatives for the mornings were used.

The VERDERER'S HALL in Lyndhurst or ALL SAINTS CHURCH in Minstead. One morning in the church I was standing in the aisle talking to the Rev. Donald Gill whilst a large party from Hythe filed in with their teachers when one boy stood by us, looked around the church, then said to Donald Gill – "Eh, mister, do they play Bingo in here?" Donald and I managed to keep straight faces!

New Laboratory

* * *

The solution to the problem was to build a large custom-built laboratory on the yard. Late autumn, the wooden garage and the lean-to shed were demolished, a large wooden garden shed was erected between the office block and the bank to house all the garden tools, the petrol-driven Flymo grass cutter, and the wooden work bench.

The brick and concrete base, with water and drainage piping and electric conduits was constructed for a 1000sq. ft. rectangular wooden building; one long side edging the bottom of the field bank, the other facing the dormitory block – this had wide, shallow steps leading down from double doors to the yard. At the far end facing the side of the office block was a single door.

Another rectangular base, backing on to the old toilet block, would be divided down the centre, the half nearer the boundary hedge with sliding doors would be garaging for a car, the other half a livestock unit with double doors facing down towards the gates.

With the two bases completed by the Southampton building firm a building surveyor/inspector from a Midlands firm came to assess and measure the work. All was correct. In two days time our sectional wooden buildings would arrive.

The next tea-time a large van with a 6-man assembly squad plus their equipment arrived; they looked around, then went off to their overnight "digs" in the locality.

At 8.00am next morning they were on the yard with their gear, their van parked by the ford.

Then, at 8.30am a long articulated lorry, loaded high with wooden sections, was carefully backed up on to the yard, its rear by the garage/livestock unit to be. The lorry, from Vic. Hallam, wood building specialists of Nottingham, had driven down overnight to the Forest to arrive on time!

It had been carefully and precisely loaded in Nottingham. The items on top of the load were the first to be needed on site at Minstead, the bottom items on the load to be the last needed at Minstead! By dusk that day both of the buildings had been erected with the roofs rainproofed.

The large glazed window units arrived the next morning. Completion by the end of the second day: doors, external cladding, guttering and downpipes all fitted and connected. A marvellous feat of organisation.

Now the local building firm did the internal work, the plumbing, the electrical sockets, built-in benching/cupboards and internal decoration, etc. Moveable cupboards/benchtop units arrived – we would be up and running for the residential season.

The two long sides were filled with window units, the two shorter, solid, walls were covered with pin-boarding above bench top height with high-level shelving for storage.

To the left of the large doorway was a waist high locked cupboard unit in which was a Calor gas bottle: on its work surface a double gas tap unit for use with Bunsen burners etc. Round the corner a large, deep, rectangular porcelain sink had teak draining boards on either side, was serviced by cold water tap and hot-water from a large, wall-mounted electric hot-water cistern.

Going along this wall were three Observation-top egg incubators. Each week poultry eggs were placed in an incubator so that a batch of eggs hatched each Tuesday during the residential season. The hatching process watched with amazement as the chick pecked its way out of the egg using its EGG TOOTH. When the chick had dried, it was transferred to our big table-top brooder, that protruded from the bank-side wall, to drink from the little water fount and, when the food from its internal food sac that it was born with had been used up, to peck bought "chick crumbs" from a shallow trough.

Beyond the incubators the bench top was occupied by the Tropical Fish aquarium, the cold water aquaria and the vivaria tanks.

* * *

The OBSERVATION BEE HIVE was bracketed to the bench top on the bank side wall, so that when a plywood window –cover was removed the children could observe the bees working, spot the marked Queen and watch the Workers walking through the glass-topped alley-way to go through the lab. wall on to the external alighting board from which they flew off on their missions; it was fun watching the pollen-laden Workers returning into the hive and storing it in cells around the brood nest.

Near the single lab. door we had a two-sided, multi-shelved book shelf unit on wheels, (that I had scrounged!). It held a large selection of children's Natural History recognition and information books and also a staff reference section.

Microscopes were purchased – one orthodox high powered model for staff use and twenty-four Binocular Microscopes for children's use: after comparative testing we selected Russian-made binocular microscopes of 12.5 magnification – ideal for children observing live specimens from the Fleetwater Stream – each instrument in its own wooden, lockable box and stored in the under-bench cupboards.

* * *

A full-time Laboratory Assistant was appointed whose duties also included looking after the new LIVESTOCK UNIT where a strong, wide, varnish topped benchtop ran along the inner wall – under it was storage space for bales of straw and hay, bins of dry animal food.

On the opposite side was a 3 storey, double hutch commercial rabbit unit. Each hutch had two compartments, one for sleeping with a hole leading to the day compartment that had stout wire windows into which external drinking bottle and food tray could be fitted. In the event of severe winter weather all our rabbits and guinea pigs normally in their arks on the front lawn could be brought into the warmth of the livestock unit.

The bench section nearer the door had animal ration charts, and a single arm lever balance where children weighed out food; any poultry eggs were weighed, before the shell texture and colour was described.

Children's luggage was stored at the far end of the livestock unit from Monday to Friday.

* * *

Extra bunk-beds in the dormitory, with the dividing door pulled right back, gave us accommodation for 24 children. Many schools sent two adults, so a teacher's bed was installed in the corner of the small room nearest the entrance gates: a hospital cubicle-style curtain rail with floor length curtain gave an element of privacy.

* * *

We were allocated an elderly minibus with seating for twelve plus three adults on the front bench seat: now we could ferry our school groups to our chosen study sites. I, my deputy, and the lab assistant all had to pass the special Hampshire driving test. I was allocated a Forestry Commission "gate key" that unlocked any of their gates in the Forest.

Still, we could only accommodate one sex at a time: most schools took a two-week booking with us.

To overcome this problem, a two-part solution was arrived at:

- the construction of a two-storey brick built dormitory block on the school field
- the purchase of the field next door from Mrs Strange

Plans were prepared by the Architects Department – the dormitory block would cost £30,000.

Mrs Strange agreed to sell the field to us and the price agreed by the Education Dept.

WOE BETIDE – the plans unravelled! The H.C.C. Treasury Dept. decided that they would not afford £30,000 for the Dormitory Block!

Many weeks later Mrs Strange advised me that, as she had not heard from the Treasurer's Dept. she had assumed that we no longer wanted the field, had bought more dairy cattle and needed the field for her livestock! I rang our Deputy Director, Mr Birtwistle who fumed, then said "Mr Gibbons, keep on good friendly terms with Mrs Strange: one day, in the future she may sell you the field". I waited 20 long years before I was able to purchase the field for the Centre – the money was paid immediately!

* * *

Our new laboratory gave us ample space in which to interest our wet day Winter season Day Visitors of up to forty children. Rabbits and Guinea Pigs would be brought into the Lab. in their lightweight metal observation cages. On fine days, after their lunch, the day visitors came into the lab, sat in a large semi-circle whilst we "demonstrated" the features of a rabbit to them.

The beautifully marked Old English buck rabbit, Elgar, was the one we usually used. Wearing our white laboratory coats, we sat seated on a chair with Elgar on our lap sitting on a waterproof sheet – he always wee'd on the ladies, but never on me – I wonder why?!

Paddy Maskell was our first Lab. Assistant – very hard-working and efficient. His home was in Pennington, Lymington: he caught an early bus to Goose Green, Lyndhurst where he removed his bicycle from "over the hedge" in the roadside field and cycled out to Minstead. On the way home, he "parked" his cycle over the hedge again.

One morning, as he retrieved his cycle, two policemen suggested that he dealt in stolen cycles! He told them his story – I received a police phone call at breakfast time – yes, I could corroborate his story! He arrived, shaken a little while later.

He had been "parking" his cycle over the hedge within 30 yards of the last private house – where the Police Inspector lived!

I arranged for him to park his cycle in the driveway of a friend of ours who lived further along Goose Green.

CHAPTER 10

STONEY CROSS AND ANSES WOOD

During the 1939-45 War "R.A.F. Stoney Cross" was an operational aerodrome on the level plain land between Stoney Cross and Fritham. Fighter aircraft and Wellington bombers operated from there.

When I first explored the area in the early 1970s the Forestry Commission had had the concrete of the "runways" and "taxiingways" removed to leave the hard core/brick base exposed, some 3 inches lower than the surrounding land. I was fascinated, over the years, to watch the recolonisation of the rubble areas by plant communities.

* * *

In the South Bentley and North Bentley Woods there were still to be seen the large circular "aircraft parking bays" with big metal hooks embedded in the concrete to which aircraft would have been tethered during stormy weather.

* * *

The one-mile long runway going in the South-Westerly direction had been reduced in width to provide the concrete based road going S. W. towards Linwood.

Butchers' Broom

Married Trees

At the S.W. end of the old runway a car-park had been constructed on the South side and also one on the North side by the side of Cadman's Pool and Anses Wood.

Deep excavations for stone/gravel had been made in the war-time: a natural spring fed water into the excavation from the runway end, thus forming a pool: this had been dammed at the far end so that a deep pool was formed with a small island in the middle that had been colonised by plant life, including small pines, birch and willow trees.

This pool was named after the recently retired Deputy Surveyor, Arthur Cadman – CADMAN'S POOL. Because of the depth of water in places, bathing was not allowed and there was a rack of life-belts by the side of the car park: "break the glass with the metal hammer to get one"!

* * *

Walking down a forest roadway into ANSES WOOD one reached a large flat area that had been graded during the war: on this the F.C. had established a barbecue site, rented out by the evening. It was discontinued after one season as parties made the habit of throwing their bottles, etc. as far as they could into forest vegetation below!

* * *

The roadway led through ANSES WOOD to join another that led, over a piped runway water drain that discharged as a fast flowing brook into the valley below, to the old taxiing strip by South Bentley Inclosure. Here and there on the edge of the woods were the brick and concrete remains of airfield defence "ack-ack" anti-aircraft sites, reminders of the by-gone age.

I followed the top track back towards the car park. On the left was a shallow pool containing a variety of aquatic plants and edged with SUNDEW. Both dragonflies and damsel flies flew over the pool and bred there.

My "irregular circular" walk through and round Anses Wood showed that there was a wealth of visual and tactile experiences to excite top junior children. I would develop it as a Minstead worksite for both my Summer Day Parties and residential groups.

There would be Teachers' Courses here before the Easter Break: their proposed activities for their day were submitted to me for prior approval. Anses Wood would be exclusive to Minstead: I was to exercise a degree of supervision, usually in the form of a lunch-time visit accompanied by my dog!

* * *

Before the first school visit my staff and I spent a whole day collecting litter from the Wood: the largest item, a practically buried milk crate still containing some full bottles. We placed all the litter in and next to the two large F.C. bins by the car park. I rang them next morning: their lorry collected.

Each school party knew that every item of their waste went back to school – a part of children's education.

Every Friday tea-time my dog and I walked and inspected the site: our reputation with the F. C. was at stake – we valued it immensely.

One Friday tea-time, Fife, my Labrador, and I stood under the big oak trees at the edge of Cadman's Pool and watched a perfectly marked male grass snake swim from the shore to the island – no doubt to look for and savour eggs of water birds, ducks and geese, that nested there.

A sight I would never forget!

* * *

I conceived an "I-SPY TRAIL" around my "irregular-circle" route starting by a track cross roads near the car park.

On the left was "THE LAZY TREE" – a beech that had got lazy and had put two branches down on the ground like elbows.

Further down the slope, on the other side is a clump of BRACKEN FERN. The large leaves called FRONDS would unfold out of the ground in Spring, grow to their full height, then die off and become brown in autumn. NEVER try to pull a frond – their edges are as sharp as a razor and cut your fingers!

Near the corner is a large YEW TREE. Look at the TRIPLETS – three medium sized Beech trees growing side-by-side out of the ground! FEEL their smooth bark. Probably three beech seeds germinate side by side.

Go to the HOLLOW BEECH TREE. With one hand in the tree, the other outside, estimate the thickness of the BARK. The thick bark is holding the tree up; is the tree still alive? – look for leaves higher up. Tiny tubes in the bark take water up to the leaves, and other tiny tubes bring sugary food down from the leaves to feed the roots.

Follow the track. Can you see two trees that have got MARRIED? Half-way up, a branch from one BEECH tree has grown into the trunk of the other BEECH tree!

On the corner where we meet the other track are several large GORSE bushes. The leaves are short and sharp and are called NEEDLES: they protect the bush from being eaten. Sometimes in winter hungry ponies nibble off the ends of the shoots! Look to see where green pods of seeds have developed from old flowers – They are like tiny pea pods. When brown and ripe the pods burst open and throw the seeds away from the bush.

Look down the valley to see a DEER PLATFORM built into a small oak tree. The Forest Keeper goes up onto the platform to watch the deer as they graze: they do not see him for they never look upwards! The Keeper knows all the deer in his part of the Forest by watching them from a number of platforms.

Deer Observation Platform

The edge of the pond has some tiny plants called SUNDEW. Why do you think they have this name: They catch very tiny insects as their "food"!

On the other side of our track is the bottom half of a rotting BEECH tree: look to see large fungi growing out of the trunk, like brackets – they are called BRACKET FUNGI and their roots are "eating" the rotten wood of the tree. What is the colour of the biggest Bracket fungus: How wide is it?

These HOLLY trees have prickly evergreen leaves. Count the number of PRICKLES on a Holly leaf. Then count the prickles on 3 more leaves on a separate branch. Have all the leaves got the same number of prickles?

Look at the KNOBBLY TREE – What sort of tree is it?

Stand still and look further along the track. Can you see the PIG TREE? The trunk has a Pig's Face sticking out from it! Now go to it – draw the face! What sort of tree is it!

Opposite it is The bottom of an oak tree that blew over many years ago. The tops of the giant roots that snapped off as they came out of the ground have become dried and brown with age. FEEL these hard old roots.

At the end of the track is a clump of small evergreen bushy plants: they are called BUTCHERS' BROOMS! The leaves that you see are not really leaves but are side stems doing the work of leaves! Carefully FEEL the pointed tip of a "leaf" with your finger. (See Appendix 1).

In early summer tiny white flowers appear on the middle vein of the "leaves". Tiny green berries develop from the flowers: they turn red when ripe.

Can you find out why these plants are called "BUTCHERS' BROOMS"?

Below the opposite side of our track is the "WOUNDED BEECH TREE". In August 1968 some thoughtless campers lit their fire close to the trunk of the tree.

The heat killed some of the bark. Fungi destroyed the dead

bark. Wet has got in through the wound and the inside of the trunk is rotting away.

Look at the new bark that the tree has grown to try to cover the wound. FEEL it gently. (See Appendix 2).

These thoughtless people have probably taken 50 years from the life of this lovely Beech tree.

* * *

REMEMBER. Look after all the animals and plants in the NEW FOREST.

* * *

To the west side of the track from Anses Wood to South Bentley Inclosure, close to Anses Wood, was an 8ft high specimen of a rare tree – ALDER BUCKTHORN. The seed for this tree probably came from bird droppings.

Botanically – Fragula Alnus – a deciduous tree growing to 4 to 5 meters in height, branches ascending at an acute angle to the main stem and dividing into long and short shoots: it has black bark. Leaves are oval shaped, 2 to 7cm long set in opposite pairs on the twigs. Flowers borne on young wood are small 3mm and inconspicuous but the berries ripen from green through white and red to black. The leaves are shiny green turning to yellow and red in Autumn.

This water-loving tree yields charcoal of exceptional value for "slow fuses".

Large quantities were grown in World War 2 near Eyeworth Pond in the New Forest to provide charcoal for the clandestine gun powder factory that was there!

Nowadays it is found growing in two places in England – Wicken Fen in Cambridgeshire and the New Forest.

* * *

The MAIN RUNWAYS of the old R.A.F. Stoney Cross provide an interesting geographical feature: they provide "WATER DIVIDING LINES".

The S. W. runway, the road to Linwood, is a "Water Dividing Line". Rain falling on the South side of the straight road drains Southward into "HIGHLAND WATER" stream that flows through the Forest to Brockenhurst where it becomes "Lymington River" flowing into the sea at Lymington.

Rain falling on the other side, the North, of the road drains Northwards into DOCKENS WATER, that has risen in the Bentley Inclosure: this stream flows Westwards, past Holly Hatch Keepers Cottage, via Moyles Court ford to the Avon, thence to Christchurch.

The other main runway is the road from Stoney Cross to Fritham. Rain falling on the East side of this road runs past the old Water Tower to become BARTLEY WATER, thence to the River Test and Southampton.

These two "Water Dividing Lines" in fact form a letter "T" on the airfield!

CHAPTER 11

ALL SAINTS CHURCH

All Saints Church sits on a knoll at the top of Church Lane from the centre of the village. The substantial LYCHGATE guards the entrance from the lane. It is built of forest oak and has a tiled roof: twin oak gates open outwards to the lane, to prevent animal access to the churchyard, and between these gates is a long, chest-high, level "table top" on which coffins are rested on their way into the church.

The LYCHGATE to a church was the "Lieing Gate" where the coffin of a dead person was "blessed" and "welcomed" into the church for the funeral, burial service.

Just inside the gate, to the left grows a large, ancient YEW TREE: part of the trunk, from where the major branches emanate, is hollow. An attempt has been made to plug this hole with concrete.

In Medieval times yew trees were the source of wooden bows from which to fire arrows: the shoots were supple and would spring back to the original shape. A village had to have at least one yew tree from which to make its bows. The problem was that yew leaves are poisonous to animals – Commoners' animals. The yew trees had to be grown where the animals could not browse them: the only place in a village that was fenced was the Churchyard, and so it became the custom to plant yews inside the churchyard – away from the animals!

* * *

Gillian, with Sandra and John, walked up the footpath from the Centre to the church. The three church bells were ringing as they walked through the Entrance Porch into the church.

The Church was nearly full: it was Harvest Festival and the Font had almost disappeared under the fruits, vegetables, flowers and sheaves of corn arranged there.

A sidesman ushered Gillian and the two children to a tiered seat in the Transept from where they would have an excellent view of the proceedings. The lowest key bell now tolled – the 5 minute bell – to remind latecomers that the service would soon be starting.

The porch door was closed and the Rvd Clifford Rham came out of the Vestry to take the service. The "3 decker pulpit" was used: the church clerk read notices from the lowest tier, the lessons from the Bible were read from the middle tier, whilst the serman was preached by Revd. Rham from the top tier. Music for the psalms and hymns was played on the harmonium.

The Revd. Rham, standing in the Porch doorway, had a long conversation with Gillian and our two children. He welcomed them to the church and said that he hoped they would attend the special FAMILY SERVICE that he had started.

On arriving home all three were bubbling – Gillian was most impressed by Revd. Rham and had fallen in love with the church – Sandy and John excited – yes! they would be going to the children's Family Services.

The church "family service" became a regular feature of our lives, the trio attending whilst I stayed at home with Jane: when old enough Jane attended the family service and became known as "the incorrigible Miss Gibbons"!

Other families attending included the Walkers from Cadnam, the Mellersh family from London Minstead and the Tippetts from Bartley. With the backing of Rev. Rham the idea was conceived of a club for young children, based upon the Family Service: it would be open to all children living in

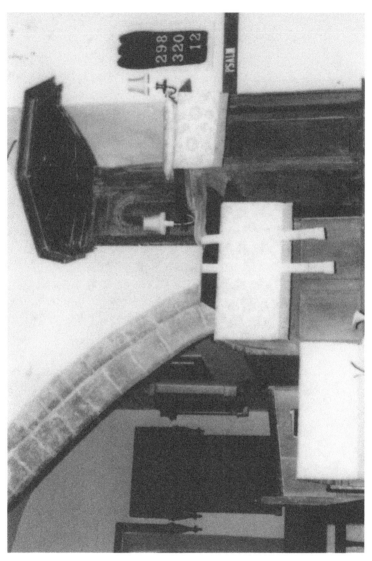

3 Decker Pulpit

Buster and Me

Minstead Parish and to children from outside the parish who attended Family Service. All would be of Junior School age. It was decided to call this club "JUNIOR MINSTEAD".

On a Saturday morning in the lounge of the School House a meeting discussed and approved a suggested constitution for the new club: a few days later it was taken to the solicitors in Lyndhurst who thought it fine.

Officers for the new club were Gillian Gibbons as Chairman, Ann Walker as Hon. Secretary, Nick Mellersh as Hon. Treasurer: committee included Wendy Tippett.

At the annual Parochial Church Council meeting in the Spring of 1969 Gillian Gibbons was elected to the council – the youngest member by at least 20 years! Subsequently she was able to interest the older members in the Junior Minstead Club and from whom offers of assistance, venues and facilities were to be made during the next few years.

* * *

"Buster", our RHODESIAN RIDGEBACK dog, was becoming elderly. He was our dog in Rhodesia – when walking with him in Bulawayo people would say what a good example of the breed he was.

The breed had been evolved by a famous Big Game hunter, Selous, during the nineteenth century. He needed a pack of fearless dogs who would flush lions out of cover so that he could shoot them. In his "mix" he put imported Bulldogs, Bull Mastiffs, Greyhounds, together with a hardy native dog from the coastal area that had a ridge of hair on its back that ran in a reverse direction: this native breed subsequently died out.

In Buster one could see traces of the ancestry – the head of a Bull Mastiff, chest of a Bulldog, slimmer hindquarters for speed from the Greyhound and a large ridge of reverse hair down his back! He stood 28 inches high at the shoulder and weighed 96lbs. All meat and bone – no fat!

Buster had travelled the 1000 mile journey from Bulawayo to Cape Town in a dog's compartment in the guard's van of the South African Railway train. The journey lasted 2 days/nights and two hours. He was placed in an "export" kennel on the top deck of the "Athlone Castle" Liner: I was allowed to exercise him on the next deck down at 6.00am each morning of our 12 day voyage to Southampton.

His feet were not allowed to touch English soil: his kennel closed, it was hoisted by crane on to a railway wagon for his journey to Hounslow Quarantine kennels where he spent 6 months in quarantine before being allowed to join us in Wantage.

We decided to buy an English bred Ridgeback puppy. The breed society in the U.K. had decided on specifications for the breed, registered at Crufts: all dogs would be judged against their specification.

We reckoned that Buster would have scored a "minus quantity" if judged at Crufts!!

I went to Brill where the top breeder of Ridgebacks had their kennels. I bought a bitch puppy, perfectly marked: they told me that I must "show" her in the future as she was of championship potential! Her grandfather was "Hunter of Owlsmoor", the national Cruft champion whose photo appeared as the breed specimen in all the top dog books.

On a good puppy diet she grew rapidly and became a "one-man" dog, her choice. Even as a lolloping half-grown pup she insisted on sitting on my knee, when I was sitting in my armchair in the lounge, and almost squashing me! Victoria, her name.

One Saturday morning, shortly before he retired, Revd. Rham came to have coffee with us. He sat in my armchair, with his back to the window, sipping his coffee. Gillian had not latched the door into our dining room: suddenly a lolloping puppy raced into the lounge and leapt into the lap on my chair –

except it was Rev. Rham and the coffee spilt over his suit jacket! Victoria removed, he dried himself with his handkerchief and a towel.

With a fresh cup of coffee he said – "Don't worry, these clerical grey tweed suits absorb everything – it will never be noticed!"

A tall, well-built man, he had been very athletic when young: rugby had been his game. With a parish in Southampton that included the University, he regularly refereed university rugby matches.

He had had a large parish in Bournemouth: from there he brought to Minstead his special ADVENT SERVICE – "The Service of Five Candles" that celebrated the five major festivals in the Christian Calendar. As each event is celebrated in the service, a group of children process from the tower, up the aisle bearing a large, lighted candle that is placed in a candelabra in the transept. Each candle has a special insignia attached to it. Sandra helped escort a candle up the aisle in our first year here.

On retirement the Rev. Rham entrusted the future of this service to Gillian: she has kept her promise to this wonderful man who retired to Cornwall where he became an honorary canon at Truro Cathedral.

CHAPTER 12

SOME MINSTEAD HISTORY

Living in Compton Cottages at the end nearest the Old Rectory lived a Mrs Purkiss, a war widow: in the middle cottage lived Mr and Mrs Purkiss – he worked in the carpentry and tools section of Pink and Stretch the hardware shop in Lyndhurst.

* * *

Purkiss is an old Minstead surname: several Purkiss tombstones in the churchyard are dated in the 17th Century.

Further back in history the Purkiss name is linked to the story of William Rufus. In late July 1100AD. William Rufus (the Red-haired King, son of William the Conqueror) was staying in Malwood Lodge, a wooden hunting lodge at the top end of Minstead. He and his party of friends were enjoying several days of hunting in "The New Royal Hunting Forest".

The story relates that on the morning of 2nd August an arrow fired at a stag by a courtier, Walter Tirel, glanced off the trunk of a tree and fatally wounded William Rufus. Tirel (Tyrell) rode to the coast, took a boat to France, and never returned!

* * *

Henry, younger brother of Rufus, rode to Winchester, thence to London to be crowned King Henry I.

What happened to the body of the unpopular late King? A local man – "one Purkiss, a charcoal burner of Minstede, was instructed to convey the body of Rufus to Winchester where it was buried in the grounds of the cathedral". To this day roads along the route are still named Rufus Way, Rufus Road, etc.

* * *

A memorial stone in Canterton Glen marks the spot of the shooting: to stop people from sharpening their knives on the stone, it is now enclosed in a metal case on which the story is inscribed.

* * *

In recent years it has been claimed that the event took place near Beaulieu.

However, I believe that much History is passed down verbally from generation to generation: this was true in Africa where I lived, and I think this applies also the Minestede story.

* * *

During the mid 19th Century several important people resided on the fringes of Minstead village. Lieut.-General Robbins, later Major-General, lived at Malwood Cottage, Mr Thomas Couchman at Malwood Lodge, whilst Mr William Preston owned Minstead Lodge and adjoining parts of London Minstead. Mr Couchman held the important position of "assistant to the Deputy Surveyor of the New Forest".

* * *

Purkiss gravestone 1680

Carrier's Cart

Practically the whole of the rest of Minstead village, save one or two privately owned plots and dwellings, were owned by MINSTEAD MANOR ESTATE, the seat of the COMPTON family: Mr HENRY COMBE COMPTON was the squire and resided in Minstead Manor House, described as "a large and handsome mansion in an extensive and beautiful park".

A younger brother, Rev. John Compton, M.A., was rector of Minstead Church and lived in The Rectory.

The Squire of Minstead was PATRON of Minstead Church: the "mother church" also of Lyndhurst Church and Emery Down Church.

The Compton Family "coat of arms" was displayed on the church notice boards.

The estate Land Agent, Joseph Fowler, lived in the Old Cottage, opposite the Rectory.

Occupations of the villagers included: a coal dealer, blacksmith, wheelwright, builder and carpenter, boot and shoe maker, bakers and grocers, charcoal burners and a wooden shovel maker. There were many farmers, most renting plots and properties from the Manor Estate.

* * *

There were two "carriers", Henry Simmonds and John Broomfield whose carriers cart went to Southampton on Tuesdays and Saturdays.

A typical carrier's cart would have been pulled by two horses: it had two rows of bench seats at the front, bench seats at the side, a large space for goods and double doors and steps at the rear. A cart would seat at least 12 persons.

The cart would leave Minstead early in the morning carrying villagers and the produce they had to sell in a Southampton market. At the end of the day the cart returned with the people and the goods they had purchased in Southampton.

* * *

During 1897 a new feature appeared in the village of Minstead. Documents show that on 27 May a piece of land, part of plot No. 391 on the 725000 Ordnance Map, was sold by Minstead Manor Estate: on 1st June an agreement was made by the County Council on the one hand and 3 Trustees on the other, for the erection of a Room for the purpose of Technical Education. The three Trustees were H.F. Compton, John Jeffreys of Canterton Manor, and Rev John Compton, Rector of Minstead.

It would seem that the erection of the Room was to cost no more than £120 and that the cost not exceeding £60 was to be spent on the provision of Cookery, Laundry and Woodwork appliances.

Boys and girls of the Parish, leaving school at 12 yrs old, would then be able to learn Technical skills at THE ROOM that would, if girls, improve their chances of obtaining work in the "Big Houses" of the area, if boys to obtain work in "estate carpentry".

Thus began the "Old Technical School", now divided into the two Crofton Cottages.

* * *

We became very friendly with the elderly Mrs Sybil White who lived in Seamans Lane: her late husband had initiated and run a bus company that had served much of the local area. As a girl she had lived in the Old Cottage where her father lived: he was Land Agent for the Minstead Manor Estate.

She related how the Squire, Mr Compton, had returned from a holiday on the French Riviera and had then summoned the Land Agent to the Manor House. To raise money to pay debts some properties on the estate would have to be sold!

Charcoal Burning

Rufus Stone

* * *

Thus began the process of organising the great sale of properties in 1921. To quote from the catalogue:

OUTLYING PORTIONS OF MINSTEAD MANOR –
FOR SALE BY AUCTION ON
SEPTEMBER 6th 1921

To summarise – there were 83 lots for sale.

Each lot was described under the headings:

Lot No: Holding: Tenant: Area, Acres: Rent: Tithe Rent Charge: Timber Valuation: and Full Forest Rights.

A definition of Forest Rights was added:

"FULL FOREST RIGHTS including rights of Pasturage, Pannage and Turbary. The Agister's Fees are 2s. 6d. per head for Cattle, and 4d per head for Pigs.

Turves may not be sold"

To give an example from the catalogue:

Lot 11 – Acres Down Farm – Alfred Peckham – 13.001 acres – Rent £22.0.0 – Tithe "£1.7.0.: Timber Valuation £0.8.0: Full rights.

* * *

The wide variety of Lots included Holdings, Farms, Cottages and Gardens, Pasture Fields, Arable fields, Building sites.

At the Auction Sale not all lots were sold, but the sale realised a total of £9675.

* * *

Of particular interest – Lot 11, Acres Down Farm sold for £925 to Waller.

Lot 16 – "Enclosure of Pasture Land" – 1.83 Acres – sold for £180 to Major Darling; on this site was erected for him Acres Down House in 1922.

In retrospect it could be said that THE GREAT SALE of 1921 opened up Minstead to the building of freehold owner-occupied properties that we see today.

CHAPTER 13

SOCIAL LIFE

During the 1960s there was an "OVER SIXTIES CLUB" that met regularly in the Village Hall. Elderly residents of the parish spent the afternoon chatting, enjoying an occasional talk, followed by a "sit-down" tea. A small group of younger ladies, led by Mrs Beryl Tear of "Oaklands", organised these afternoons. On two winter afternoons in 1968 and 1969 I was pleased to give them talks, illustrated by slide transparencies, on my experiences in Southern Africa.

* * *

Junior Minstead had settled down with a regular pattern of events. In the beginning, a member of the church, Mr Clark, a carpet manufacturer with a factory at Wilton, had invited the club to use facilities at his property, "Stonnard" near Stoney Cross. Parents took the children there to play tennis on the courts and to swim in the swimming pool.

* * *

The committee of the Village Hall gave permission for the club to have free use of the large room at the Hall. Junior Minstead met every Tuesday tea-time between 5pm and 7pm. Gillian Gibbons and her team of helpers provided children with light refreshments, e.g. biscuits and squash, and a range of activities .

Besides games, several village people taught skills, e.g. basketry by Miss Tomlinson of "Fylingdales" and art by Jeanie Mellersh. Country Dancing was taught by Mrs Sybil White who played the piano accompaniment.

Maypole Dancing: Gillian had purchased a pole and set of ribbons and after tuition, the children gave a Saturday afternoon performance on the Village Green near the shop, with Mrs White providing the music. On the second occasion Steve Cattell had got the Hall piano on to a farm trailer and taken it to the shop car park and Mrs White sat on the trailer and played the piano!

Football for the boys was played on the outfield of the Cricket ground at Football Green, encouraged and tutored by several fathers. Jim Coffin organised at least one match against boys from another village.

* * *

A Sports Day was held at the Cricket Club ground with a variety of races for boys and for girls – sprints, egg and spoon, sack, three-legged, etc. There were events for Mothers and for Fathers: I won the first Father's sprint race, having been given a 5 yard start because I was over 40 years of age! Refreshments and a barbecue helped to make it a very enjoyable Saturday afternoon. The event was repeated more than once.

* * *

Winter time and November Bonfire Night – Junior Minstead was invited to go to the home of Mr and Mrs Robinson of Eugenie Cottage, just below the top Village Green. On their field adjoining the house a huge bonfire had been built. Parents and children watched as the bonfire, with "effigy" on top, was lit: sparklers were given to children. Whilst the fire burned down, hot drinks were served.

Finally a firework display was put on by a visiting pyrotechnics expert ending with rockets. Three cheers for the Robinsons – a most enjoyable event, to be repeated in subsequent years.

* * *

Christmas was Pantomime time. A motor coach full of children and adults went to see a Pantomime at the old Salisbury Playhouse – a traditional type of pantomime. I was put in charge of two boys whose parents did not go: sitting in our block, with one on either side of me, the three of us had a very enjoyable evening with ice creams, etc, in the interval – no problems!

* * *

Short plays were enacted at the club: the great energy and enthusiasm of Nick Mellersh led to the production of the first Junior Minstead Pantomime in the Village Hall. In later years the pantomimes were developed and expanded under the direction of Nick.

* * *

The Minstead Cricket Club had been the generous hosts to Junior Minstead. They had good pavilion facilities, well cared for and maintained. The club had applied to the "Lord Tavernors" for a grant towards the improvement of the two dressing rooms.

The real mainstay of the Cricket Club in those days was Jim Coffin who lived just across the road from the cricket ground. He was busy coaching his two sons to become members of the team. Practically all the players in the 1st XI and in the occasional 2nd XI were from the Minstead area: there was a full fixture list against teams from the area.

Maypole Dancing

On a Saturday or Sunday afternoon there could well be 50 spectators: a collecting box for club funds was passed around. Teas for the teams were organised by lady family members.

* * *

The club owned lawn mowers and rollers, kept in a locked shed next to the pavilion. According to the "Lease" the outfield had to be opened up for a period during the winter so that Commoners' animals could graze there: the "wicket square" was securely fenced during this period and it usually received a treatment of "green conditioner".

During the long cricket season, the wicket square and the outfield were kept in first-rate condition. Minstead Cricket Club was a club to be proud of.

* * *

At the Study Centre I had created a large sandpit in the front garden near to the now fenced off road gate: here John and Jane would spend happy times. A regular passer-by who always had a word with them was Mr. Kempton, the groom to Miss Pultenay's horses, who rode a beautiful chestnut horse along the road past us every day.

* * *

When not in use a large plastic sheet was pegged over the sandpit to prevent animals, especially cats, from using it as a toilet!

There were two large Yew trees on either side of the Centre front garden, one by the sandpit/gate area, the other in the roadside hedge near to the double entrance gates.

The Yew by the sandpit was a MALE tree and in early February its tiny flowers produced clouds of very fine Pollen that blew away on breezes. The Yew by the entrance gates was a FEMALE whose tiny flowers were pollinated by the clouds of white/grey pollen from the MALE tree. These flowers then produced tiny fruits that became BRIGHT RED BERRIES by mid-September – these berries contain highly poisonous seeds that pass through the digestive system of birds that eat them!

* * *

One February the skin on Jane's face suddenly became red and blotchy. We took her to see Dr. Danby – no idea what the cause was – we had not beaten her! With treatment her facial skin recovered.

The next February we realised that she had been playing in the sandpit whilst the clouds of pollen were being blown around. The pollen had gone on her face and affected the skin – she was allergic to Yew pollen!

* * *

Reg Long lived in a green painted house in the vicinity of Grove House with his wife and young son. A tall, strong, dark-haired man, Reg had served in the Eight Army throughout the long and costly siege of Monte Cassino in Italy: it was a point in his life that he would never talk about.

He regularly drove his elderly blue Fordson Tractor, plus trailer, around the corner by the Centre: another person who always waved to our children. He always smoked a pipe. We always looked for two plumes of smoke when Reg rode by – one from his pipe, the other from his tractor exhaust pipe!

CHAPTER 14

LIGHTNING STRIKES

The Churchyard of Minstead Church was a place full of interest.

The Lychgate, built in 1938 of forest oak by a local firm of builders, commemorate the 90 years of continuous service to the Church as Rectors by 3 members of the Compton family. The first was Rev John Compton, a younger brother of the Squire, who was Rector for 56 years: he died in 1898.

* * *

Taking the path to the left of the main entrance path, there are interesting GRAVES/ TOMB STONE.

Some wealthy people attempted to foil "body snatchers" who stole bodies from graves and sold them for medical research!

Near the E. Chancel end of the Church is a large, secure tomb. On a heavy stone base is a strong rectangular stone box in which the coffin sits: on top a large white stone slab. To further ensure safety it is surrounded by an ornate iron fence! (see illustration).

Nearby is the headstone of a little child's grave: it bears a small coloured portrait, and below is inscribed a poem.

* * *

By the hedge bordering the East of the churchyard is the "FAMILY SQUARE" of the CONGLETON family. Among their graves is one of a family relative, Percy Turnbull, who was a

Fenced Tombstone

Musician's Grave

composer: on his gravestone is inscribed an extract from one of his compositions.

* * *

To the South of the Church is the large "FAMILY SQUARE" of the COMPTON FAMILY, the Squires of Minstead Manor: this SQUARE is surrounded by white stone kerbing.

* * *

There are several graves of SERVICE PERSONNEL who were killed in the 1939-45 War. They are marked by white headstones erected by The War Graves Commission.

* * *

The church building was extended to the South by building the TRANSEPT in 1790: this necessitated removal of a section of the South wall of the NAVE: to prevent ceiling collapse a cast iron pillar was erected to support the roof timbers.

The Transept was built by Minstead Manor to house estate workers in the wooden box pews. At the rear was the SQUIRE'S PEW covered in a red material: there he and his family would sit for the services.

The 1790 Transept was extended to its present length in 1825 and had a single width double-door in the South East corner through which the Squire would enter.

* * *

During the 18th Century it was the custom of Church Masons, when erecting buildings or extensions, to carve a small head replica of the MONARCH and to tuck it under the eaves.

Queen's Head

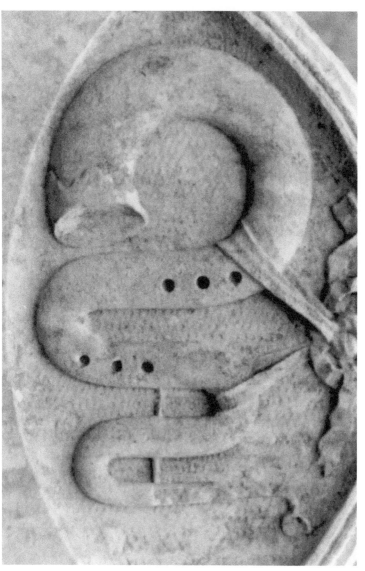

The Serpent

Standing in the churchyard, looking at the West side of the Transept, one can see a tiny sculpted stone "Lady's head" tucked under the eaves at approximately the South end of the 1790 building. The Monarch at that time was "QUEEN ANNE"!

* * *

Below this point, by a pathway is the headstone of Thomas Maynard who died in 1807 aged 27 years. He was a soldier in the South Hampshire Yeomancy.

He also played an instrument in the army band. The instrument was a "SERPENT": this was a wind instrument with finger holes to produce different notes – (as you do in a similar way with a Recorder). His regiment had a "SERPENT" carved on the headstone.

* * *

An amateur musician from Chandler's Ford made a working model of a SERPENT. We persuaded him to visit Minstead Church to play his SERPENT accompanied by some friends playing other period instruments.

* * *

Near to this headstone is a YEW TREE – not like the Common Yew by the Lychgate – but an "IRISH YEW" of a more columnar shape. A "sport" of the Common Yew that was found growing in Ireland in Co. Fernanagh in 1780.

* * *

Close to the South Boundary of the churchyard is a medium-size OAK TREE. During the mid-1930s it was struck by lightning during a thunderstorm: the result was a vertical slit in the bark of the trunk on the side facing the Church. The cambium layer gradually healed near the slit, but it left a 2-inch vertical scar on the trunk.

One Friday afternoon, Mid-Summer in 1969, I had been to the bank in Lyndhurst and had collected my children, Sandra and John from the Primary School. We drove home via Swan Green and Emery Down where we encountered heavy, thundery rain. Then, as we neared the bottom of the rise to Robinsbush Cross Road, there was a blinding flash of lightning with near instantaneous boom of thunder. THAT WAS CLOSE!

Safe at home in the School House, Gillian said that she was in the kitchen preparing our meal when the lightning and thunder happened – it was very close!

Next morning we learned that the Oak tree in the Churchyard had been struck. Another vertical slit in the trunk bark – a few inches away from the original 1930s slit!

* * *

Almost under the spread of this Oak tree is the large grave of SIR ARTHUR CONAN DOYLE with that of his wife. He had died in 1930 at his home in Windlesham: he was buried in the grounds of his house. We understand that some years later the family decided to move from the house, but the problem was where to take the coffin that was in the grounds.

However, at one stage he had lived in a house just off the Cadnam to Brook road, in Minstead Parish. The family requested that his coffin be buried in Minstead churchyard. Jack Whitehorn, the gravedigger, related to me how they had dug the grave space: a dawn private burial, just the family, no rector, no service, as he was not a Christian.

* * *

The large HEADSTONE of dark stone is inscribed:

"Knight, Patriot, Physician and Man of Letters."

Looking at the inscriptions with parties of my young school visitors, I would question the items.

Yes! We know what a KNIGHT is – a "SIR!

PATRIOT – someone who would die for his country.

PHYSICIAN – a medical doctor who would get you better if you were ill.

MAN OF LETTERS – a difficult one – with prompting LETTERS – words – sentences – stories – a writer of stories, books – an AUTHOR!

* * *

Then we would turn our attention to the Oak tree trunk with vertical scars from the lightning strikes. They would feel the bark and the scars.

"Now, there is a saying – 'LIGHTNING never strikes twice in the same place!" Do you think that is true?

* * *

An Oak tree – A tomb – and Sherlock Holmes looking on!

CHAPTER 15

SOME CHURCH HISTORY

As you enter the Church from the porch be careful of the stone step: it is uneven, having been worn away over the centuries by the countless millions of feet that have entered this church.

The oldest part of the church is the FONT. Let us pick up its story. One day in 1890 when the gardener at The Rectory was digging deeper than usual as he prepared a site for the planting of some new shrubs. His spade struck a large piece of stone: working carefully round the stone he realised that it was the top of a special, large piece of light coloured stone.

So the gardener, Mr H. J. Abbot went to the Rectory to tell the elderly Rev. John Compton of his discovery. The Rector went into the garden to inspect the find. Two men from the nearby cottages were fetched to help unearth the object. It was an old font!

After much deliberation by the Squire, and the old Rector the old font was eventually taken by horse and cart to specialist church stone-masons in Winchester where it was cleaned.

Returned to Minstead it was reinstated in the church for use in baptisms.

During 1969 I talked to an elderly descendant of H. J. Abbot: he confirmed the accuracy of the story.

* * *

The Church Font

How had the FONT come to be buried in the village? In the mid 17th Century the government of "Commonwealth Protector", Oliver Cromwell, decided that churches in England should be quite austere places, devoid of beautiful objects or paintings. Most churches had large, colourful mural paintings of Biblical scenes covering their walls: these were used in the teaching of the scriptures to parishioners, most of whom were illiterate.

The paintings in Minstead church were obliterated, save for a portion of coloured painting high up on the wall that was between the nave and the chancel: it has been hidden from view by a large beam and false wall above the high stone arch above the entrance to the Chancel. Whilst roof/ceiling repair work was being undertaken in the 1970s the then agile Rev Tim Selwood crawled along the inside of the bare roof and, with the aid of his torch, gazed at this piece of medieval wall painting.

* * *

The wall paintings attended to, what of the FONT? With its carvings on the sides it would not pass the scrutiny of Cromwell's men, so it was discarded, to be replaced with a plain font.

It was taken down to the village. I imagine that the men charged with disposing of it knew the font – they and their families had been baptised in it – it meant a lot to them – so instead of destroying the font they dug a deep hole and, in darkness, buried the font on land that eventually became the garden of The Rectory.

* * *

How old is the font? In 1973 the Rev. Donald Gill escorted into the church a group of C. of E. antiquarian experts. They looked at the font and said that it was a Saxon font!

Iron grave markers 1969

Bed-head or Leaping Board 1969

With the further spread of Christianity during the Anglo-Saxon period one may imagine that in the first instance a simple Oak Preaching Cross was erected on the knoll above the settlement of Minstede. Later, a simple church erected there would have an oak frame, wattle and daub walls and a thatch roof: in it would have been placed the stone font carved with symbolism figures.

* * *

The Normans who built the present church built in stone with local rubble in-fill – a simple rectangle – our "nave" – with a thatch roof. In it was housed our historic font. Our Norman Church was probably constructed during the 12th Century.

The List of Rectors in the Church Porch dates from the early years of the Norman church. The first named is one "ROBERT": I used to imagine him as a pious bachelor preaching to and caring for the parishioners of Minestede.

But were my thoughts about a pious priest tending to his flock of parishioners in the New Royal Hunting Forest village of Minestede correct?

It would seem from old records that our priest Robert had a taste for venison, the Norman King's venison. During his time at Minestede he had paid a large fine and also had served a prison sentence for his venison ventures!

Robert had a son, also named Robert, who lived on the Isle of Wight as well as in Minestede. He had also faced charges of breaking the strict Forest deer hunting laws!

Like Father – Like Son!

* * *

The Transept is, in many ways, the Squire of Minstead Manor's part of the church. On the wall is a large plaque relating to the last three male Comptons: they all died within 3 months of each other in 1943. The eldest, the Squire – Henry Francis Compton – born in 1872 was the last to die: he had been Squire of the Manor and a Verderer of the Forest for many years.

Sadly, he had no direct male Compton heir. His only son, Henry Richard Compton, a Lieutenant in the Coldstream Guards, died on 21st November 1923 – a young man.

In his memory, his father – the Squire, commissioned the design and creation of the large stained glass window that dominates the South end of the Transept – the "Saint George's Window". It was said that the face of Saint George resembled that of the Squire's late son.

* * *

The heir to succeed Squire Compton was a descendant through the female side of the family – Peter Green.

When the 1939 War began he was in the Army with the B.E.F. in France. Fighting against the German Blitzkrieg break-through in May 1940 he was very severely wounded. He was posted as "Missing, believed killed".

For many months there was no further news of him. The saddened, elderly Squire organised a Memorial Service, to remember him, in Minstead Church.

Later, news filtered through from the Red Cross in Switzerland, that a young, badly wounded officer, Peter Green, was alive.

As the Rev. Donald Gill said to me – "Not many people have a memorial service to them whilst they are still alive!"

Peter Green affirmed that his life had been saved by the skill of a Belgian Surgeon in a Belgian Field Hospital during 1940.

He visited the Studies Centre on several occasions and was fully supportive of our efforts and activities. I asked if he could provide me with any information about the early years of the

Compton Dynasty and the Manor. He was unable to but knew that there were some boxes of old documents in the attics of the Manor House. If they were ever to be examined in the future, he would let me know.

Squire Green was a regular attender of Matins services at the Church and would enter via the Squire's door at the South end of the Transept, then sit in the red plush Squire's bench seat.

As Patron of the Church he was very supportive of the Church Wardens, especially during inter-regnums, the period when we had no rector and a new one was being sought. My wife, Gillian, was a Churchwarden for 25 years, a post of much responsibility and hard work!

Leaving at the end of a Matins service in 1979, I became sandwiched in the aisle by the two Churchwardens – Jack Collins and David Davies. "We need a new Church Treasurer – you would make an excellent Treasurer, Stanley – what about it?!" Thus, I became Church Treasurer, a post that lasted ten years!

CHAPTER 16

ROUND AND ABOUT

The road system around Cadnam had been re-drawn after the 1939-45 War. A round-about had been constructed at Cadnam: this linked the often congested A31 from Ower, Winchester and the North, the A336 from Totton and Southampton, and the A337 through the Forest to Lyndhurst. The A337 had originally run from the old Cadnam cross-roads, through what are now the grounds of Bartley Lodge Hotel, fringing the Cadnam Cricket Club ground to join the Minstead, Bartley Cross roads.

* * *

The volume of motor traffic increased during the 1960s. The flow of traffic along the A337 was often slowed by Commoners' animals that had the right to roam over the road. Many a summer day saw long queues into Lyndhurst caused by the large group of ponies, standing nose to tail across the entire road enjoying the shade of the tall trees overhanging the road by the new POLICE STATION!

* * *

The Highways authority had one solution: the entire length of the CADNAM to LYNDHURST road was fenced to prevent animals having access to the road. The MINSTEAD-BARTLEY cross roads was widened to facilitate overtaking at the junction.

Cattle Grid

Underpass

A wide loop of road was constructed where the Bartley Post Office road joined the A337 thus giving drivers good visibility of the junction: The old, straight section of road was ripped up and reverted to Forest land.

* * *

All the junctions of the minor roads had a full road width CATTLE-GRID fitted. By the side of each grid a wide wooden gate was constructed: this would allow horse-drawn vehicles to access the junction.

* * *

The increase in traffic on the A31 Trunk road led to the Highways Authority building a second carriageway: it became dual carriageway from CADNAM to RINGWOOD with UNDER-PASSES at certain points to allow animals and horse riders to cross under the A31 road.

There were problems at the Ocknell Area below Stoney Cross: piles driven in the ground to provide foundation got no purchase – the sub-soil was probably wet shifting sand. After several weeks the road engineers evolved a solution to this expensive problem: old fashioned, deep layers of baled heather and deeply driven concrete piles.

* * *

Several forest side-roads that had had junctions with the A31 were eventually blocked off. A large concrete bridge was built to take the A31 over the Bolderwood to Linwood road.

* * *

A bus service provided an alternative to cars for MINSTEAD residents. A regular service from Southampton to Ringwood via Totton and Cadnam had a stopping point at CASTLE MALWOOD on the A31. People walked up the village to catch the bus, whilst those coming from Southampton got off at Castle Malwood and walked down the hill to the Village!

* * *

A limited single-deck bus service went up through the village to Castle Malwood then back down through the village to Lyndhurst. The small number of people using this service resulted in a reduction of frequency: finally the service ceased altogether when the Council subsidy was withdrawn. To this day, a taxi is the only alternative to the private car for Minstead residents wishing to travel further afield!

* * *

The junction of the MINSTEAD road and the A337 had been originally well below the top of the hill on the LYNDHURST side. Several serious accidents occurred when vehicles going from Minstead to Lyndhurst were hit by vehicles speeding over the brow of the hill. The junction was moved to the brow of the hill from where it is possible to see A337 traffic coming from both directions: lengthy slip roads were made on either side of the new junction.

* * *

The Stony Cross cross-roads on the A31 was closed after a series of accidents, with long slip-roads constructed on either side. A small cross-over road from one carriage-way to the other, to the West of the Compton Arms was closed. A reflection on the increasing speeds of motor traffic?

There remains, in 2018, just one junction near the top of Malwood Hill, that allows vehicles, especially those from the S.E.B. Castle Malwood depot, to cross from the West-bound carriageway to the East-bound carriageway.

About two-thirds of the way up the mile long hill from CADNAM to MALWOOD is a minor junction leading to the tree-lined Running Hill road to upper Minstead Green. It used to be a two-way junction – both exit from, and access to the West-bound carriageway. On occasions drivers, especially holiday makers, when reaching the junction from the Running Hill road made the mistake of turning right – into the on-coming Westbound traffic coming up the hill – sometimes with serious consequences.

To prevent this egress, both Parish and District Councils lobbied the Highways Authority to alter the junctions: this they did by making the final section of Running Hill road one-way only.

With the addition of a 6ft 6ins width restriction sign now-a-days only cars and light vehicles can leave the A31 at this junction.

How the internal combustion engine has altered the FOREST!

CHAPTER 17

THE CENTRE
IN TOP GEAR

By the mid 1970s the Centre was running at full capacity.

Residential capacity for 24 boys or girls per week with one or two accompanying adults was booked for the whole summer term, barring the last week, and, for six weeks during September and October.

OPEN DAYS, for the children and their families were held on the afternoons of the Saturdays preceeding the end of the Summer Term and the October Half-Term.

On Open Days the LABORATORY was filled with examples of the children's work whilst the last hatchings of chicks were in the brooder. The cooks provided refreshments in the dining-room: donations went to our general expenditure fund.

* * *

During most weeks of the SUMMER TERM schools from all parts of the county made use of the ANSES WOOD study site on the edge of the old Stoney Cross airfield going directly there in their hired motor coaches.

The "lead-teachers" of these parties attended a Teachers' Day Course at the Centre held during the last two weeks of Spring term. A slide-illustrated talk introduced the Forest as an "educational resource" with special emphasis on ANSES

Laboratory Open Day Displays

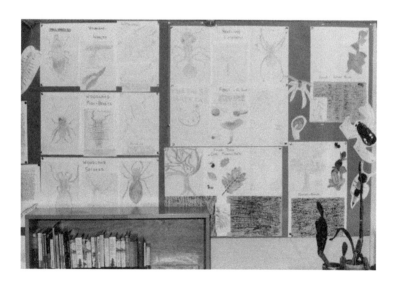

WOOD. Clips of relevant notes and specimen work sheets – e.g. Tree Study – together with pages of outline animal footprints and mammal droppings were given out. Our home-made clinometers were tried out to measure the height of tall trees at the Centre.

An early lunch, then, in convoy we made our way to ANSES WOOD CAR PARK. Here I made a most important point – no children should be set to do studies in the vicinity of the car park!

The previous year I had driven into this public car park one lunch time on my way to visit the Day Party working in Anses Wood. From my car I noted that a pair of boys were very busy working under the tall trees some 20 yards from the car park: no others in sight, no supervising adult either. However, standing on the edge of the car park was a middle-aged man watching the boys intently.

After a few minutes I got out of my car with my dog and walked across the car park towards the boys: the man hastened to his car and drove off swiftly before I could note his car number plate!

The lesson – beware of paedophiles in the Forest!

* * *

A walk with the teachers around the suggested Nature Trail, then the exploration of mini-environments such as heathland-bog, the shallow dragonfly-pool, the woodland floor, by which time the "magic of the environment for creative work" has become apparent.

Farewells in the car park at the end of a busy day, but not before reference to the two large Forestry Commission litter bins as a reminder – "you must leave the worksite even clearer of litter than you found it"!

At least 2 weeks before their visit each "lead teacher" sent me a copy of the proposed programme of events for my approval.

To comply with my agreement with the Deputy Surveyor "to exercise some supervision" I visited each school group at Anses Wood for at least an hour in the middle of the day.

I witnessed interesting sketches and paintings done by children as well as prose and poetry writing evoked by this wonderful environment.

Friday tea-time – a quick walk around the Wood with my dog to see that all was "spick and span" – our reputation with the Forestry Commission was most important!

* * *

DAY VISIT parties came to the Centre during the whole of November and most of the second half of the Spring Term: a party consisted of an entire class with their teacher and accompanying adult per every eight children.

A typical day. Arrival by coach 9.45 – 10.15am: in groups to the toilets and issuing with our quarto-size home-made varnished clip boards.

Coach to park under main-road beech trees near Robinsbush Cross Rds. In groups, the first led by my deputy, walking slowly along the I-Spy Nature Trail from Robinsbush Cross Roads, down the lane, over the ford footbridge up to Acres Down Car Park. N. B. Never go close to a New Forest Pony!

Make sure we see the Witches Brooms!

* * *

Back to the Centre: toilet, wash hands in the porch then sit in the Laboratory where served with picnic style lunch including a warm home-made "Cornish style pasty" – orange squash to drink.

Toilet if required, then gathered round to see a rabbit, usually ELGAR the "Old English" – demonstrated.

Charles, Buff Back Gander

Dutch Rabbit – Jan

Indian Silver Pheasant – Rajah

Golden Pheasant – Ming

Then jackets on and with clip boards, round the field path to look at our collection of ducks, geese and poultry with at least one outline picture to colour in with questions to answer.

* * *

Finally, toilets, clip boards collected and on coach leaving us usually 2.30-3.00pm.

Beforehand I visited every Day Visit Party in their school and, with the aid of my boxes of slide transparencies talked to them about the Forest, the Centre and especially about all our named animals.

On one visit to a 3rd Year Junior class at a Waterside Junior School I had been asked how old were Charles and Petunia, our Buff-Back Geese. I told them and had added that I thought their birthday was on the day of their visit the Centre.

I had forgotten all about this, but on the day of their visit I was fetched from the office to witness the whole class process up the field path to the Goose run where they hung a huge home-made BIRTHDAY CARD on the wire fence and sang "HAPPY BIRTHDAY" to Charles and Petunia!

* * *

The Centre was busy during the Mid-Winter period – the first half of December and January.

"Special Schools" would come for a day usually 10.30 to 2pm: Forest Gate in Totton and Norman Gate from Andover were regular visitors, the latter coming for one-night stays.

* * *

Bartley Middle School was local to us. During this mid-winter period we would collect a group of 8 to 10 boys and girls at

9.30am and bring them to the Centre in our minibus. A mid-day meal was provided: we returned them to school by 2.45pm. The group was about one third of a class, so over three days the whole class would have done studies chosen by the class teacher – e.g. stream animals collected then examined in the Laboratory with our binocular microscopes: our Centre livestock always featured as part of their day.

The school was two-form entry, so the top year provided us with six groups – each group came at least twice, so we were kept busy!

* * *

Domestic staff were busy – the wood floor of the two parts of the dormitory were "machine scrubbed", then given two coats of a special varnish – the annual treatment. Then access to the Dining Room was via the kitchen door.

We also found that this varnish was ideal for preserving our home-made clip boards!

CHAPTER 18

RESIDENTIAL WEEK

Prior to a residential stay at the centre much preparatory work was done so that our young visitors would have an enjoyable and memorable experience.

Before the end of the Spring Term the "lead-teachers" attended a day course at the Centre: this gave them a background of knowledge about the Forest and the range of mini-environments available for study. Each went home with a two-box Forest Resource Pack.

Several weeks before their visit to us I visited the school. With the help of slide transparencies I introduced the children to the Centre and our named animals that they would help look after: many questions asked!

If there were sizeable trees in the school grounds we would learn how to use my thick black wax crayons and grey sugar paper to make a bark rubbing. With some of my home-made clinometres we would learn how to estimate the height of buildings and trees.

I got to know the children –and, more importantly, they got to know me!

* * *

In this chapter I will portray in some detail a typical residential week of activities undertaken by a group of twenty-four boys or girls. Alternative options will be described. The normal residential domestic routines have already been described in an earlier chapter.

Monday morning arrival between 9.45am and about 10:15am, the coach backed up to near our entrance gates.

Disembarked, they stood by the dormitory wall whilst the driver helped by Paddy, our laboratory assistant, unloaded the luggage from the coach luggage holder.

I welcomed them to the Centre and introduced them to Wendy, my deputy, Paddy, my secretary and the lady member of the domestic staff who was on duty.

* * *

Within an hour all clothing and belongings had been put away, empty cases put on the yard for Paddy to stow at the far end of the livestock unit, and the yellow P.V.C macs and sou'westers taken from the numbered porch pegs on to the yard. The longer macs swapped to the taller children, Wendy demonstrated the way to fold and roll up the mac, sou-wester in a pocket; all done satisfactorily, the children put them in their own haversack and hung it on their pegs in the porch.

* * *

To the laboratory, allocated their tables by their teacher, they were introduced to all the features there especially the three incubators and the shuttered observation bee hive where bees went out through an observation tunnel to an alighting board on the outside of the lab from where they flew away to forage. The rule – only one table of 4 to the incubators at a time when invited to do so by staff or the teachers.

Next, our Monday journey into the Forest. The first 12 children plus the lead-teacher loaded into the minibus to be driven via Robbinsbush cross-roads to a gateway on the top road to Stoney Cross: the locked gate was under the solitary Scots Pine tree opposite the track leading to several houses and down to The Grove.

All the Forestry Commission gates in the Forest had identical heavy-duty padlocks: The Forestry Commission key fitted all the padlocks in the entire forest! The Centre had two of these numbered keys for which we had had to pay a deposit: with them we could open any gate – padlock in the Forest!

Unlock, drive-through, lock the gate behind us, and drive on! Along the forest track to forest track cross-roads where the group disembarked to walk along a track as far as the oak Bee Tree. The minibus returned to the Centre to be loaded with the second group, the second visiting adult, the box of clip-boards and equipment and, most importantly, the boxes of packed lunches and containers of diluted squash. I usually went with the second group on a Monday.

* * *

Picnic lunch under the shade of big trees within sight of the Pony-Round-Up Station. Empty bags, plastic cups collected, boxed and put in the minibus, Clip-boards given out – no signs that we had been there!

The Pony-Round-Up Station: the use explained, then a mock "drift" with some children being the "mounted Commoners" driving the other children – the "ponies" through the funnel into the large holding pen: some "ponies" put through gate to the branding pen! Any signs of wood fires that heated branding irons, on pony tail hair cut off during tail marking?

With grey sugar paper and wax crayons rubbings of the brand marks tried out on the wooden posts and rails.

* * *

Then to the gate into the PUCKPIT INCLOSURE, noting the ditch-bank-wire fencing. Our September visitors would see Bee Hives just inside the Inclosure fence under the shade of the large Pine trees: beekeepers buy a permit from the Forestry Commission to place hives of bees there during August and September in order to collect a crop of Ling Heather honey.

Down the track to BARNEY'S BEECH – the amazing old pollarded Beech tree! A change of Forest Law over 300 years ago forbade the "pollarding" of Forest oak and beech trees, a measure to preserve them for future naval timber. This meant that Barney's Beech was pollarded BEFORE that date, i.e. it is well over 300 years old.

Why were the trees pollarded ? To cause them to grow a large number of "shoots" at the top – about 10 feet up from the ground. These shoots would provide fencing poles and also green leaves for the Commoners' animals to eat.

The "shoots" on Barney's Beech developed into sizeable trunks growing out of the top of the main trunk.

These "trunks" are now being attacked by "BRACKET FUNGI", especially the old main trunk. It is shaped like a "bracket", the sort of thing that holds up a shelf at home!

How many "trunks" growing out from the main trunk? What is the colour of large "Bracket fungus" – it is "eating" away at the inside wood of the big main trunk.

I wonder how many people have walked or ridden under this tree during the last 300 years? What sort of clothes were they wearing?

* * *

Now we walk up the wide grassy "roadway" – called a RIDE – wide enough for Forestry Commission vehicles to drive along, including fire-fighting Land Rovers. The young trees in the plantation are LARCH – notice the spirals of "leaves" growing out of the twigs – they turn yellow in September, then fall off – "deciduous" trees – look for old "cones" on the ground – they released seeds when ripe.

Fire Beaters

Fire Break

At the top of the Ride is a wide gate with a large spring fastening. To the right of the gateway, inside the fence, is a large notice warning about FIRE: By it is a rack of FIRE BEATERS – what is a "beater" made of?

Outside the gate the heath plants are mown short – it is a "FIRE BREAK" to stop forest fires from spreading from woodland into the valuable plantations of trees inside the Enclosure. How many of your stride will measure the width of the firebreak to the path on the other side?

A walk along the path to the partly hollow young oak tree to feel the width of the bark by putting one hand inside, the other outside the trunk. To the minibus and ferrying back to the Centre.

* * *

MONDAY AFTERNOON – and the introduction to the Centre animals that are adopted for the week. Two pairs of children at a time were collected by me from the Laboratory and taken to the Livestock Unit. Here we consulted the ration chart to see what food had to be fed to our poultry animals in the afternoon. A scoop from the food bin – layers' pellets or mixed corn – and the correct amount weighed out on the big Lever-balance. With the rations in the food tins we went to the stand-pipe in the toilet block, got small zinc water buckets and half-filled them with water.

Then the slow walk up the path to the run where our poultry lived. Alberta and Ontario, the pair of Canada Geese were the first to be attended to. Unbolting their gate, going in, hooking it shut behind us, the mixed corn ration was emptied into their long zinc food trough. Then to the zinc water fount – this was emptied and the fresh clean water from our bucket put in it. Food and water given, out through the gate, to stand and watch them for a few minutes whilst the other two children went into the next run to meet their animals.

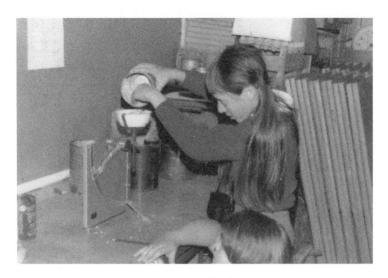

Weighing Food

Feeding

Looking for Eggs

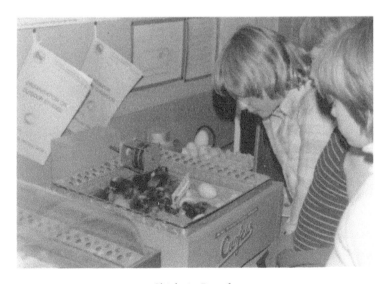

Chicks in Brooder

Dandy, the Bantam cock, and his hens were given their ration of Layers' pellets, their water fountain emptied and re-filled, then the really exciting part – had they laid any eggs? Unlatching the double nest box unit at the side of their poultry house we peeped in – there were three eggs, two in one nest, one in the other nest – the nests had a dry-sawdust base with dry hay on top forming the nest. The eggs carefully picked out of the nests and put in our empty food tin.

After a few minutes, we went back down the path to the Livestock Unit – empty buckets put away, then each egg was weighed on the balance, the weight recorded. We felt the shells to discover what the texture felt like: we recorded this, and its colour and weight on our clip board. Eggs on the big cardboard collecting tray so everyone could see them – then back to the Laboratory.

* * *

Simultaneously Wendy, my deputy, had 4 children at a time to go to the front lawn to learn to look after the named Rabbits and Guinea Pigs. They took a bucket with water and tins with the ration of the compound Rabbit pellets that they had weighed out on the balance.

First of all the ark had to be moved one space downhill on to fresh grass: the floor of the ark was covered with wire netting – they could not scratch up the lawn, but could eat the grass under the netting!

The big roof of the run part of the ark was raised, the rations put in the heavy stone bowls and fresh water put in the stone water bowls: a section of a carrot was usually put in the run. The run lid, covered with wire netting and plastic sheeting was lowered back in place.

Wendy would lift the felt covered roof of the sleeping quarters so that the nest could be examined – dry sawdust base with a straw nest. At one side of this compact nest was a hay rack – replenished in the morning by Paddy, the lab assistant.

He moved the arks in the morning, washed the stone bowls and fed green stuff – cabbage etc. from the kitchen, and sometimes wild plants he had gathered.

* * *

On TUESDAY AFTERNOON as soon as their animals had been fed, all children went back up the field path with their clip boards, etc. to do the study sheets about their animals: these sheets had an outline drawing to be coloured in and a series of questions that required careful observations to complete the answers.

Time was found during the remainder of the week for everyone to see all the animals and choose another study sheet to do.

* * *

MONDAY EVENING after tea was the time to learn about the INCUBATORS. A tray of 24 eggs had arrived from a poultry keeper friend. I carefully marked them with a very soft lead pencil - a large CROSS on one side of the egg, a large "O" on the other.

All eggs in the incubators were "turned" twice a day: Paddy turned them with the "O"s uppermost at breakfast time: I turned them to show that "X" uppermost at bed-time. When a hen wanted to raise chicks she went "broody" and would sit in the nest box all day and start to "cluck"! If she were given a "clutch" of 12 or 13 eggs she would sit on them to "incubate" them with her body heat. At least twice a day she would turn the eggs over, so that the developing chick (embryo) would not stick to the inside of the shell.

Chicks in Incubator

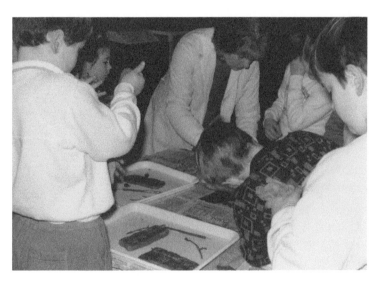

Plaster cast technique

Minibeasts Under Microscopes

With our incubator we imitated the broody hen, and turned the eggs!

* * *

Our empty incubator had been cleaned and the Thermostat on the heater set. Tomorrow morning this new set of eggs would be put in the incubator by Paddy. Twenty days later some chicks would start to hatch.

How would the chick hatch out of the egg? By now it had grown a tiny hard piece on the top of its upper beak – this was its "egg tooth". With the "egg tooth" it would tap hard on the inside of the egg shell to crack it, working round until it had cracked over half-way round the shell. Then it would push its feet on the other side of the shell so that its head came out of the shell and it could then crawl free!

Its damp body would dry out so that the "down" would keep its body warm. It would not need to eat for at least twenty-four hours because, before it started to hatch, the "egg yolk" had been drawn up inside its body – this yolk was its food.

The "egg tooth" would disappear after a few days – absorbed into the beak.

When several chicks had "dried out, we would place them in the "BROODER" where the special lamp provided warmth just like the mother hen would, and they could sip fresh water and peck at the specially manufactured "chick crumbs".

I took the insulating material cover off the incubator that had chicks due to hatch, so, two at a time, the children could peep through the clear plastic incubator lid to see if any eggs had "cracks" appearing – "Yes! Three had!" By after breakfast tomorrow we should see some chicks in this incubator! Something to look forward to on Tuesday morning!

TUESDAY MORNING. Yes, chicks had hatched in the incubator! They would be in the brooder by tea-time.

PLASTER CASTING of animal footprints to be done in the Forest this morning. An introduction to the apparatus – an enamel dish and table spoon, a strip of flexible clear plastic, and a bag containing "Plaster-of -Paris". Water bottle. Then a demonstration – a Fallow deer front foot imprint on a plasticine base – the plastic strip clipped to make the "former", sealing the outside with plasticine (mud in the Forest). The careful mixing of P. and P. and water in the dish – pouring into the "former". Perhaps a second mixing required.

Then to the Forest, minibus parked near the entrance gate to Highland Water Inclosure. Twelve children looking at the big trees – "height" measurement with "clinometers" -"girth", at shoulder height: minibeasts under the trees and nearby leaf litter.

* * *

The other twelve, armed with their Plaster casting kit walked down towards the little forest stream. Keeping on the grassy side of the sloping path we looked in the soft clay of the centre of the path for footprints. Yes – a selection – Fallow deer, ponies, cows.

Six selected and the pairs of children prepared their "former", sealed with mud "Is that okay?" "Yes you may start and mix and pour". All done, then back to the minibus with their kit.

Swap over – the other twelve went to plaster casting, the first lot doing their tree study.

Picnic lunch in the shade near the minibus.

* * *

Then a walk past the plaster casts, over the little stream bridge and through a Forest gate to an area that had been "clear felled". A section had been re-planted with conifers: this section was surrounded by a 6ft high wire netting fence to prevent the deer from browsing off the tops of the young trees.

Plaster Casting in Forest

Using Clinometer

Rubbing Norway Spruce

Bark Rubbing

Further along we turned on to a wide grass-covered forest ride. On one side were a cluster of SWEET CHESTNUT trees now in flower: though tall, they were bushy having been "coppiced" to produce a crop of fencing poles that would be slow to rot.

On the other side of the road was a plantation of mature NORWAY SPRUCE trees with very attractive bark patterns and large, long old cones that could be found on the ground. So bark rubbing with thick black wax crayons and grey sugar paper.

Back on the ride, we came across teams of large ants on foraging expeditions. They were carrying their trophies back across the ditch to a huge mound just under the first row of spruce trees. The mound about 3 feet high and 4 feet diameter was covered with old dry pine needles: it was a WOOD ANT NEST. The workers entered through holes in the side of the mound to go deep underground in the nest.

A fascinating story to tell about the Queen ants laying many eggs in galleries deep down in the nest.

* * *

The walk back out of the Inclosure, over the stream bridge to stand by our plaster cast. Staff ease out the plaster cast, scratch children's initials on the top: walk back to the minibus with casts and equipment – all to be put to carefully into boxes.

Back in the laboratory the casts are placed in trays to dry and harden off, a drink, then feeding and studying the animals.

* * *

After tea the group usually walked up Fleetwater Hill to the wide spaces of the Manor Waste and played rounders or football before supper, showers and bed!

WEDNESDAY – going to ACRES DOWN CAR PARK, climb up the steep slope to the ridge at the top. A wonderful view over the Forest – the woodlands, plantations, heathlands, and in the far distance the reflections from motor vehicles on the distant A35 road from Lyndhurst to Christchurch and Bournemouth.

The teachers have chosen from several possible studies:

1. PLANTS and MINIBEASTS on the Ridge: effect of heavy rain eroding the ground to form little "ravines".
2. Plants and minibeasts on the sloping HEATHLAND.
3. The transition from the Heathland to the bog – special plants – e.g. BOG COTTON grass and the "insectivorous" SUNDEW plant and other plants of the marshland.

A member of staff would insert depth measuring poles into the bog to demonstrate the gradual deepening of the bog – Strictly OUT OF BOUNDS!

* * *

PICNIC lunch back on the ridge during this period.

Ferry back to the Centre, a drink, sorting out of the morning's study work, followed by animal feeding and studies.

* * *

BEFORE TEA TIME – taking twelve children at a time by minibus to Minstead Manor Farm via the Lodge gateway on the Emery Down Road – where there was always a notice outside "Beware of Adders" – perhaps to deter tourists!

To the MILKING PARLOUR to watch the dairy man milking cows with the suction milking machines. Finally a sip of freshly cooled milk from the dairy

* * *

THURSDAY and visiting teachers had selected a variety of studies to do, after their pre-season study days at the Centre.

A WOODLAND STUDY below Acres Down Bog. Trees and bushes adapted to the wet environment: the densely covered willow "CARR" where we saw the little forest stream emerge from the bottom of the bog: and saw unusual leafless little plants – a variety of mosses, liverworts and fungi.

A VILLAGE STUDY, often combined with a "CHURCHYARD STUDY", both carefully marshalled by staff especially if walking up the village street.

* * *

Victoria, my Ridgeback, had been "speyed" (neutered) by the vet when old enough. She had grown up to be a Cruft's standard bitch, a beautiful looking animal.

I never had any intention of "showing" her – she was the dog to guard my family, the replacement for "Buster" who had been "put to sleep" at 13 years of age with an "inoperable" growth in his neck. He was buried at the top of the field near the roadside hedge. I planted a young oak over his grave: "Buster's Oak" has grown into a lovely tree that is thriving there today.

Victoria, alias "Vicki" or "The Lady V" was a "one-man-dog" who would have given her life for me.

Several times on a Friday morning I was fetched from the Laboratory to take Victoria into the house: she had been sitting quietly at the top of the yard guarding the Centre. The delivery men from Rank Hovis had refused to come through the gate with their trolley to deliver sacks of flour to the Centre kitchen. Victoria had not said a word, had not moved, but just looked at them! They had got the message!

In the Forest with me she guarded the school groups. One morning, on the top of Acres Down, I was with pairs of boys who were doing a minibeast survey: Victoria stationed herself just

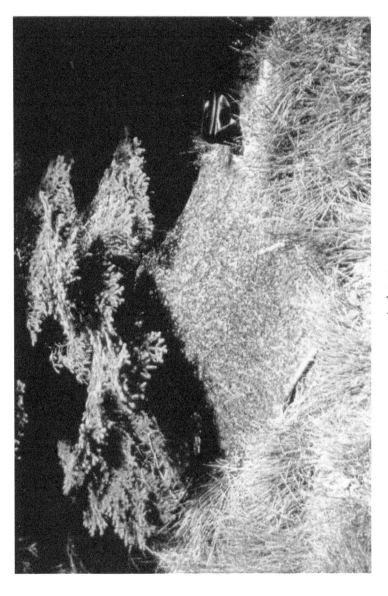

Ant's nest

beyond the furthest boys: people coming up the path noticed her expression and diverted away from us!

* * *

THURSDAYS: some teachers chose to do a Village Study, some a Churchyard Study combined with a Village Study.

Double box Resource Boxes on Church Studies and on Village studies were loaned to teachers. These contained sets of my slide transparencies together with sets of mounted photographs and sets of notes about many items and places of interest.

Around the Village Green items of special interest included the plaque outside the Old Technical School, the date stones set in the brickwork above the doorways of the Village Shop 1768 and The Old Cottage 1728.

The real attraction was the large painted plaque of "The Trusty Servant" under which was the white board on which, in black lettering, was the explanation of why he was a "Trusty Servant."

A carefully shepherded walk up one side of the village street led past the Old Court House, the Village Hall to the Upper Village Green with the circular seat around a specially planted memorial tree. From there one could see Eugenie Cottage. During the latter half of the Eighteenth Century and during the Nineteenth Century the property was a Public House under the sign of the NEW INN. By 1913 it had reverted to a private house named Eugenie Cottage.

In 1964 it was bought by Mr and Mrs David Robinson who have since made alterations to the front of it.

Further up the main road is Shovel Cottage, an old building where an ancient craft of shovel making had been practised. Beech wood, locally harvested was used to make the special shovels that were used in the beer brewing industry for turning and shovelling the malted brewers grains – beech wood did not interact with or affect the "grains".

A Trusty Servants portrail would you see
This Emblamatic Figure well survey
The Porkers Snout not nice in diet shows
The Padlock shut no secrets he'll disclose
Patient the Ass his Masters Wrath will bear
Swiftness in errand the Staggs Feet declare
Loaded his Left and apt to labour saith
The Vest his neatness Open Hand his faith
Girt with his Sword his Shield upon his arm
Himself and master he'll protect from harm

Trusting Servant

* * *

THURSDAY AFTERNOON animal feeding and studies done early, then the children were taken in our minibus via Emery down to BOLDERWOOD car park, the first group doing a short investigative woodlands trail whilst awaiting the arrival of the second group.

Then I climb up on to the public observation platform to look over the Bolderwood Farm land for a possible deer sighting.

At a certain time we came down from the platform, walked in file very quietly, through the private single gateway (Public NOT allowed) and down the grassy side of the roadway to Bolderwood Farm, to sit very quietly in the shade of an oak tree.

Then, as if by clockwork, a small green Forestry Commission van drove down through the gateway to park nearly opposite us. Out got Keeper Derek Holland, took two large bags from the back of the van: these contained special animal feed "nuts" that he dribbled on to the ground in lines just opposite to where we sat, and in an "unusual voice" "called the deer". Then he stood with us under the tree.

Out of the bushes and trees of the farm area came the deer, mainly Fallow – both bucks and does of all ages, occasionally a light coloured one, and sometimes some pairs of Roe deer.

We sat silently and watched. Quietly he would explain things to us.

The feeding complete, the deer dispersed and we walked quietly in file back through the gate to the Car Park having thanked Keeper Holland.

* * *

This visit was MY TREAT OF THE WEEK for my school parties. I had negotiated the visits with Deputy Surveyor, Mr Dom Small, some years before.

* * *

FRIDAY MORNING routines, described earlier in the book, led to a long session in the laboratory with each child having the use of a Russian built 12.5 magnification binocular microscope to study a succession of small aquatic minibeasts brought from the Fleetwater stream after the earlier "dipping" with the enamel bowls.

Study time over, the minibeast put in boxes in the sink area ready to be returned to the stream by the Lab Assistant.

* * *

Then, using the "blackboard", the message of CONSERVATION was developed.

Suppose that this aquatic fly lays 100 eggs: some will be eaten by other stream animals before they hatch: leaving perhaps 30 to develop as nymphs that we have identified by the number of tails – the Mayfly nymph has ? – Yes, 3!

Before these 30 nymphs have lived, eaten and grown in the stream long enough to emerge and hatch out as an adult Mayfly, other animals in the stream will have eaten a lot of them, perhaps as many as 28, that leaves 2, out of the original 100 eggs laid, to emerge as adult Mayflies who will lay another generation of eggs!

It is so important that when we take specimens from the stream we put them back carefully in the parts of the stream that they came from so that they may continue their life there. Mr Maskell will do that whilst we have our hot lunch.

We wave goodbye to our party of children that have spent the week with us.

I trust that they leave us having absorbed

A RESPECT FOR ALL LIVING THINGS,
BOTH PLANTS AND ANIMALS

FOR THAT IS THE MESSAGE OF CONSERVATION.

* * *

During the mid-1970s residential season, a lady writer from a monthly Hampshire magazine spent a day at the Centre.

She wrote a long article about the activities she had witnessed the visiting party of boys doing.

* * *

"Above all they have learned the words of the Warden – "a respect for all living things" which is briefly what Conservation is all about.

If they can remember all of this and fire their friends with their own enthusiasm and beliefs there is a chance that the countryside will be a great deal safer in the hands of the next generation.

If this is the case we have people like Mr Gibbons and places like Minstead Rural Studies Centre to thank for it. One wishes there were more of them.

* * *

"WOULDN'T IT BE FUN" SAID ONE INGENIOUS YOUTH, "IF THE NEXT SCHOOL SUDDENLY CANCELLED THEIR VISIT AND WE COULD ALL STAY ANOTHER WEEK!"

CHAPTER 19

EXTREMES OF WEATHER

On the front lawn of the Centre we had installed an official STEVENSON'S SCREEN: set at the correct height and aspect the slatted structure had weather recording instruments inside it.

Nearby, sunk into the lawn was an official RAIN GUAGE. A home-made WIND VANE indicated the wind direction.

Readings from our Weather Station were usually made in the middle part of the day. They were MAXIMUM TEMPERATURE, MINIMUM TEMPERATURE, RELATIVE AIR HUMIDITY, WIND DIRECTION, AND RAINFALL.

* * *

In late June 1976 a period of very hot weather commenced with very high maximum temperatures recorded.

From 25 of June we recorded twelve consecutive days when the maximum temperature exceeded 90°F: on 2 days, Sunday and Monday 27, 28, the maximum recorded was 100°F.

The hot weather continued, peaking again at over 90° on 22, 23 and 24 July.

How did this affect life at the Centre? Before the end of the residential term the dining room and dormitory windows were shut and the curtains drawn after breakfast to keep the heat out!

Early evening the curtains drawn back and windows open to allow slightly cooler air in!

* * *

The hot dry weather continued through August.

One Saturday afternoon in late August I was playing bowls at Lyndhurst Bowling Club with a senior fire officer from the Lyndhurst station who was on leave.

One after another, bells ringing, fire engines raced around the one-way street system.

"They are all out now" said my friend – and a little later – "they are bringing in engines from outside the area!"

The Forest was tinder try. A large fire to the south of the A31 dual carriageway west of Ringwood had jumped over the carriageways!

Later that afternoon a forest fire near the Ashurst camp site advanced towards Lyndhurst at a walking pace and was halted at the approaches to Lyndhurst!

THIS WAS THE DAY THAT THE FOREST BURNED!

- and it made National B.B.C News headlines. A cousin in Staffordshire rang to offer to fetch our children to safety. Minstead was safe – we had no fires in the vicinity.

The hot dry weather continued into September and the Autumn Residential season.

Then a new weather pattern arrived. During early evening the sky in the S. W. became very dark and then lightning, thunder and heavy rain ensued for an hour or two – almost subtropical in nature!

This evening pattern of weather continued for several days until eventually the weather resumed a more normal early Autumn pattern.

THE LONG HOT SUMMER OF 1976 WAS FINALLY OVER.

* * *

TEMPERATURES

1976	Max	
Weds	83	
Thurs	87	
Fri	93	
Sat	97.5	
Sun	100	26th June
Mon	100	
Tues	95	
Weds	91	
Thurs	94	
Fri	98	
Sat	95	
Sun	96	
Mon	95	5th July
Tues	96	
Weds	88	
Fri	82	
Sat	85	
Mon	83	12th July

1989	Min	Max
22 July	60	94F
23 July	63	94F
24 July	62	95F

One Sunday morning I was returning home having put my elder daughter on an early morning flight to Spain where she was doing her University Language Year.

Mid-morning as I drove down the A272 road from the A31 I noticed that the roadside trees and bushes were waving violently in a strong wind.

Arriving home, the sky at Minstead was very dark. I rushed up to the bee-hives to adjust some hive entrances and as I got back to the house the strong wind lashed down heavy rain.

This continued well into the afternoon, almost darkness and heavy rain.

The centre of this storm was to the South-East of us – almost continuous lightning in the distance.

The city of Portsmouth endured almost darkness, frequent lightning and heavy precipitation: large hailstones some the size of golf balls destroyed the panes of glass in hundreds of conservatories.

It was reported that some elderly people thought "the end of the world had arrived"!

This vicious storm was centred entirely over the Solent and Portsmouth – a one off with no apparent explanation for it.

* * *

November 1986 saw the night of the famous "Michael Fish storm". On the BBC evening news the experienced Met. Office Forecaster commented that someone had rung in to say that a hurricane was approaching – referring to his chart he forecast rain from the S. West., no way a hurricane!

At midnight I got out of bed to grasp the bedroom window that was open before the violent winds tore its hinges from the window frame. There was heavy rain and much lightning to the South whilst the wind increased in intensity.

Our Ford

Wet Friday morning

The electricity went off and later a cracking noise in the trees by the ford.

Dawn showed tree debris everywhere: looking over the ford we saw that a large side trunk had been torn right off the oak tree – it lay in the stream below the embankment.

No electricity – we were without it for a week. Fortunately, we could cook on the propane gas stove in the Centre kitchen. Paraffin wax candles were the order of the day.

Mid-morning after the storm I drove my car, evaded road closure signs and got to Ashley, near New Milton to the house that we owned there. The storm had flattened the 6ft high wood panel fence that divided our rear garden from the public footpath. With stakes and a roll of 5ft wire netting I was able to make a temporary fence.

It later transpired that we were on the Westerly edge of the storm: it drove North-Eastwards through Hampshire, Sussex and beyond wreaking havoc with trees as well as buildings.

The Isle of Wight did indeed record wind speed gusts of hurricane force!

Driving from Brockenhurst to Beaulieu through the Forest we could see Southwards thousands of acres of Forestry Commission tree plantations flattened to the ground by the winds that had come up from the coast.

A storm with long lasting effects on the landscape.

Incidentally our Centre Weather Station recorded a total of 167mm rainfall for that November.

CHAPTER 20

CARNIVALS AND FETES

A Saturday afternoon in August and the Minstead Carnival procession was due. We joined a large number of people standing on the Green and in front of The Trusty Servant, many of whom had parked their cars on the Glebe field behind Compton Cottages where the old field gate had been opened.

The previous week the Lyndhurst carnival had processed down the entire High Street with the police keeping the rolling traffic following slowly behind. Many of the floats and displays were stored for the Minstead Carnival the following Saturday. Incidentally, a few years later the build up of traffic had been so great that the Police withdrew their permission for the carnival to process down the High Street.

* * *

The sound of music and the Carnival procession began to appear – walking clowns with buckets collecting money for charities, a small decorated truck with musicians providing music, followed by a series of floats with various themes and activities depicted. Many floats were on farming trailers pulled by tractors, the people in them dressed in a great variety of costumes and hats: straw bales provided seating on these floats.

Between the floats were individual people in fancy dress walking, riding cycles, even tricycles: again collecting buckets for small change for charities.

Then, finally the sound of a real steam engine approaching blowing its whistle! Round the corner came a steam road roller driven by its proud local owner. A real feast for the eyes of all the children, the smoke from the funnel, the steering mechanism, the fly-wheel, the whistle!

Slowly it processed and disappeared into the distance! That was the end of the Carnival procession.

Much to talk about during our walk home down the church footpath.

* * *

A few years later a fete was held on the large field below Minstead Lodge that adjoined the drive that led down to Football Green.

A famous TV personality had been invited to formally open the fete. It was the TV Magician Paul Daniels. He, his entourage and the Fete secretary then toured all the side-shows and exhibits on the field.

I was participating in a sideshow run by the church. We had borrowed the Wooden Stocks: one person stood in the stocks, head and hands protruding. The competition – how many times could you hit the head in the stocks by throwing wet sponges from a distance of 12 feet? Five sponges a shilling!

It was my turn in the stocks when Paul Daniels and his entourage arrived. I was dressed in shorts and an old gardening shirt.

He missed with his first two sets of sponges, but having got the range hit me with two sponges of his third set! His magic had worked at last!

* * *

During the early 1980s Village Fetes were held on the upper part of the field that was accessed through the gateway nearly opposite the old Stable block of The Old Rectory.

Parking was on the lower part of the field whilst the events of the fete were all on the upper part of the field.

I had been asked to assist the organisation by helping to count money! I was, at that time, the church Treasurer.

Going through the little gate at the top of the churchyard near to the incinerator, I went into a small caravan where all the monies collected at the fete were taken. Yes, I would count and put into the little bank plastic bags, the small change!

Silver shilling pieces, two shilling pieces and lesser silver coins. Bronze coins, pence, half-pence and the odd farthing together with odd foreign coins!

All done – the bags of coins that the bank would accept – all checked and totalled.

I put the unusual and foreign coins in bags for a charity that traded in such coins!

After 4 hours of coin sorting and bagging I looked at my fingers and saw that the skin was starting to flake – the year before, skin tests at the Southampton Hospital had diagnosed that my skin had been allergic to anything treated with formalin, to rubber and to anything containing nickel.

Most coins of the realm contained nickel, especially "silver" coins. Incidentally, all "stainless-steel" items were rich in nickel.

I went home, washed my hands carefully, then applied to my fingers the special ointment prescribed by my doctor – it took 24 hours for my finger skin to recover from the money counting at the fete!

* * *

In recent years a Fete has been held on the Village Green during August. As a member of the church team I was involved in setting up trestle tables, a tent near the shop fence and facilities for side shows. The fete began at 11.00am and ran until 4pm. Half the proceeds were donated to the Church.

Cakes, sandwiches had been donated. Bottles of wine, etc donated to the Raffle stall where tickets were drawn from a little rotating drum.

Refreshments were sold from the blue tent during the day. Home-made cakes and garden produce sold at another stall. A book stall selling used books always did a steady trade.

Held at a peak week-end in August the fete attracted many holiday-makers including those going up the Church in search of the grave of "Sherlock Holmes" – i.e. Conan Doyle.

As a fund-raiser the fete was always successful thanks to the hard work of all the volunteers who wearily packed everything away after 4pm.

CHAPTER 21

MINSTEAD CHURCH BELLS

During 1978 an enthusiastic group of people had started to learn the art of CAMPANOLOGY – Bell Ringing.

We were a group of all ages: I went with my younger daughter Jane. We had managed to get, as our tutors, two people from Eling, Nr Southampton – MR JOHN HARTLESS, a member of The Guild of Ringers and his daughter.

We were learning the basics – how to pull the bell rope and when to let it go so as not to hit your head on the ceiling of the ringing chamber: one young lady did that, with painful consequences!

Our new District Forester, Mr Geoffrey Green had come to live in Seaman's Lane: he had done some bell-ringing previously and came to join us with his younger daughter Jo. He was very enthusiastic and was elected "Captain of the Bells"!

Friday evening, when work and school was over for the week, was the time for our bell-ringing sessions. John Hartless and his daughter usually came to the School House to have sandwiches, cake and tea with us before going up to church.

John Hartless was a British Rail official with responsibility for the large building in woodland close to the main Waterloo to Southampton line that housed retired railway people.

* * *

It had become apparent that the existing three church bells were in need of repair and rehanging. The Parochial Church Council supported this idea together with the proposal that two new smaller bells be cast and hung there to make a peal of five thus allowing ringers to ring one hundred and twenty "changes".

The P.C.C. Hon. Secretary, Mr. Michael Clarke, and I, as Hon. Treasurer, contacted several organisations stating our requirements and appealing for any old redundant bells, etc. We ended up placing the contract to the old establishes bell founders in London, The Whitechapel Bell Foundry, Ltd.

THE CHURCH BELL APPEAL was launched at a church service on Whit Sunday, 3 June 1979 with a target of raising £5,000. (See Appendix 3). The appeal was called

"LET THE BELLS RING"

Individual named donations rolled in. One "anonymous" donation arrived from Hong Kong – a couple worked there, had a little cottage at Bank and came to Minstead Church when on holiday there.

During the following 12 months many special events were held to raise money for the appeal including Maypole Dancing on the Village Green, drama and singing events in church – all listed on the balance sheet.

Events culminated with the CHURCH FETE on 26 May 1980 held on the Village Hall field (now the car park).

Many side shows and fund raising events were spread over the field during the morning.

It was a long Bank Holiday weekend and the Forestry Commission Ocknell Wood Caravan and Camp Site was fully booked. I advertised our Church Fete on the Village Hall field with a pile of hand-outs given to the F. C. officer in charge!

It was easy for the holiday-makers there to cross the A31 at Stoney Cross and drive down to Minstead. This they did in large numbers, many going for refreshment at The Trusty Servant first of all!

I had organised the Junior Minstead to wear fancy dress and assemble on the Green. I had booked the Boys' Brigade Marching Band for the afternoon.

They started playing at 1.45pm on the Green. Having drawn the attention of the visitors in the Trusty, the Boys' Brigade Band proceeded to march slowly up the road towards the Village Hall followed by the dancing Junior Minstead children: the holiday makers in the Trusty joined in the large procession to the Fete at the Village Hall field!

Entrance fees paid at the gate, the Fete field was full of people enjoying the side shows and competitions. We closed at 6.30pm and as the balance sheet shows we made an overall profit of £678.89p. (See Appendices 4 and 5).

* * *

The contract for work on the Church Bells had been signed. Many local volunteers helped to save money by taking down the three bells. Tim Fields, of Stoney Cross Road, had set up his own business: he had a small truck and offered to take the bells plus any scrappage bell metal that we had been gifted, to Whitechapel Bell Foundry in London.

Gordon Cutler arrived with his mobile crane and carried the bells to Tim's truck.

As will be seen from this final account from Whitechapel, this local work saved us a lot of money. (See Appendix 6).

* * *

It was arranged that a large group of us would journey to Whitechapel for a special day – the day our new bells would be cast!

Geoff Green and Jo, myself and Jane, Mike Clark and Rachael, Steve Cattell and his two boys, helped make up the party.

We all learned a lot about the work of the Bell Foundry and saw the molten bell metal poured into the moulds.

Many, many photographs were taken! A visit we would never forget.

* * *

The new bells were brought to the tower along with the three originals, all tuned together to provide a "peal of five" and all fittings were done by the professional Bell-hanger from Whitechapel who test rang them. He was afforded local hospitality, so saving more money.

The final account from Whitechapel Bell Foundry totalled £6,348.90p after V.A.T. (See Appendix 7).

The Minstead Church Bell Appeal account was finally closed on 23 December 1980. We had raised £8160.89, leaving us with a balance in hand of £1811.90p. (See Appendix 8).

* * *

A special service was held at All Saints Church on Sunday May 11, 1980 when the new peal of five bells were dedicated by the LORD BISHOP OF SOUTHAMPTON.

During the section – "The Examination of Ringers" the reply to the RECTOR'S question was spoken on behalf of the Ringers by Mr Geoffrey Green, "Captain of the Bells"

WE SEEK TO WORSHIP AND SERVE ALMIGHTY GOD THROUGH CAMPANOLOGY AND WE ACCEPT THE CHARGE OF THIS PEAL OF BELLS, WITH HUMILITY, IN HIS NAME.

* * *

At the close of the service the bells were rung by a group of ringers from the GUILD of RINGERS.

Minstead rejoiced to hear the maximum number of "changes" rung – one hundred and twenty-five.

* * *

CHAPTER 22

THE CHURCH
OFFETORY DISH

During the 1939-45 War the function of the R.A.S.C. – ROYAL ARMY SERVICE CORPS – was to supply the front-line fighting troops with ammunition, petrol and rations.

Most units were equipped with lorries and trailers. However, in the preparations for "OVERLORD", the landings of the Allies in Normandy, it became necessary to form a specialist unit that could land with the 6th AIRBORNE DIVISION and supply them, usually under enemy fire.

Thus a special Company was formed – the 716 Company, R.A.S.C (Airborne Light). It was in envisaged that they would go into action with their Jeeps, trailers and motorcycles, landing by glider and parachute in the midst of the enemy. Thereafter, it would collect the various supplies parachuted from bombers and transport aircraft and distribute them to the fighting troops.

* * *

The members would have to be young, fit and able to look after themselves when there was no "frontline" and you had the enemy all around you.

Parachute training was done, the 8 jumps completed. they were proud to display the "blue wings" badge on the right shoulders!

Glider training proceeded, learning to squeeze jeeps and trailers into the long cigar-shaped Horsa gliders.

Gliders were not widely available, so many parachuted into action on D. Day – a few by glider with jeeps, but many came later by sea.

The "drop" near Ranville on "D Day" (6 June) was widespread but men fought their way to their target area and set up dumps in the Divisional Maintenance area within a quarter of a mile of Pegasus Bridge over the River Orme. On "D Day +1" the various sea-borne elements began to appear and by "D Day + 6" 716 company was all together again.

Daily shelling and "straffing" kept them "out of mischief". One night the large ammunition dump was set on fire and burned for almost 24 hours during which four of "the lads" were killed and many wounded.

With the eventual defeat of the German Army in the Falaise Valley, the 6th Airborne unit took part in the pursuit of the Germans over the SEINE.

* * *

In September, a return to England by sea via the Mulberry Harbour, but sad to be leaving behind in the beautiful Churchyard of Ranville no less than 18 crosses bearing the names of "our lads" who would never again see their native soil.

* * *

Their new home was in the New Forest in the delightful little village of Minstead. The officers lived in Minstead Lodge, whilst "other ranks" lived under canvas in Minstead Manor.

New men made up their depleted ranks and training continued. They made many friends in the village, took part in village activities and had a weekly Church Parade to All Saints' Church.

Christmas at Minstead did not occur for Von. Runstedt launched the offensive in the Ardennes Forest – the "Battle of the Bulge". Two days later they were in the snowbound Ardennes helping to stem the German break-through of the American lines.

Thence through Holland to the Rhine crossing and occupied Germany.

V.E. Day – 9th May 1945: ten days later a return to Minstead to leave the village on 28 days of "embarkation" leave.

* * *

Further service in the Far East, Malaysia thence Middle East, Palestine and Egypt.

Returning to U.K. and in June 1948 the Company's brief career of just 5 years came to an end, disbanded at Cheltenham. A comparatively brief lifetime, but into those 5 years had been crammed a wealth of activity and no little gallantry evidenced by the M.B.E, two M.Cs, two M.Ms., one B.E.M and several "Mentioned in Despatches" awarded its members.

* * *

Fast forward to 1952 and the third annual Reunion dinner in London organised by Roy Day, who had been the C.S.Ms Corporal, and his committee.

They decided to raise money to buy a "Solid Silver Alms Dish" on which would be inscribed the names and dates of their "fallen comrades". This would be presented to the little church of All Saints' in Minstead, the New Forest village where they had been made most welcome in 1944 and where they had held regular Church Parades.

Thus, on 3rd May 1953 at a Memorial Service the Silver Alms Dish was presented and dedicated in All Saints' Church, Minstead. (See Appendix 9).

* * *

On each Sunday nearest D. Day, 6th June, old comrades and their families came to the Morning Service at Minstead.

During the 1980s I got to know Roy Day and his family and many other veterans including "Jock" Brennan, the officer of the Company who had written the "Reminiscences", the history of the unit: he now lived in Poole.

It is from his "Reminiscences" that I have drawn the information for this account thus far.

By late 1997 the veterans had discovered more names of late comrades that they wished to add to the Alms Dish.

By early 1988 we had arranged a "Service of Rededication" to be held at church on 5th June 1988. This would be followed by us hosting them to a sit-down cold luncheon in the Village Hall – to a total of 102 "guests" i.e. veterans and their families.

The full programme of the "Service of Rededication" is appended. It closed with the "Prayer of Airborne Forces":

"May the defence of the Most High be
above and beneath, around and within us,
in our going out and in our coming in,
in our rising up and our going down,
all our days and all our nights,
until the dawn when the Son of Righteousness shall arise
with healing in his wings for the peoples of the World
through Jesus Christ our Lord.
Amen."

The appended letter was sent to all those who had helped in the organising of the event at the Village Hall – from the 4 of us who had organised the event, John and Judith Styles and Gillian and me.

The end of the letter reads:

"Minstead means a lot to 716 Company –
716 Company means a lot to Minstead.

The Memorial Alms Dish to fallen comrades remains with us to
keep, to Treasure and to respect for all time."

* * *

I think that this letter sums up the day, and our thoughts on our
future responsibilities.

* * *

A few weeks later David Davis, a churchwarden – wartime
Royal Artillery officer and now Head of Mathematics at Totton
Grammar School, and I discussed the future.

"Stanley, in a few years time neither of us will be around:
I agree that we should arrange that the Church Flower Ladies
should have money to decorate the font on the Sunday nearest
D.Day."

The P.C.C agreed that we purchased "Undated CONSOLS",
nominally 2 ½% interest. But the price that we paid for them
meant that we would receive well over 8% annually on our
investment. Thus two half-yearly dividend payments insured
that over £80 was available each year to decorate the Font in
remembrance of 716 Co., R.A.S.C. Airborne Light in perpetuity.

CHAPTER 23

ODDS AND ENDS

One Friday mid-afternoon I opened the gates and got into my M. G. Magnette that was parked in the tree shade by the ravine hedge. Reversing to get the angle to get through the gates there was a terrific bump – I had backed into Gillie's Gig that was in the shade further up the fence!

Inspection showed not a mark on the Magnette, but the near-side front-wing of the Mini was stove-in, with the lights dangling on their wires!

* * *

Saturday morning, a quick trip to Southampton to buy spare light fittings and a spray-can of the correct maroon colour.

I fashioned the correct curve on the end of a piece of 2 x 2 inch oak post and set about beating the wing panel back into shape. The under-side cleaned and painted with rust-proofing aluminium paint. The top surface rubbed-down gently then sprayed with the paint. The light fittings replaced and by tea-time "Gillie's Gig" looked like new!

However, having worked on the wing, I realised that we were trusting Gillian and the 3 young children to a car that would crumple easily on impact – not safe enough for the family.

* * *

Next week-end we traded the Mini for a larger saloon car; a "used" Wolsley 1100 – safer for the family and more room to put shopping.

However the Wolsley proved to be a "Friday Afternoon" car. During the winter months a succession of minor faults developed – very annoying, though covered by the guarantee.

Easter and I took the car back to the garage in Brockenhurst. John Gates would take it back – no loss if I bought another car from him. What had he got?

Quite a selection but he had a large saloon that would keep the family safe – a semi-retired coffee planter on long leave from Brazil had bought the car in the Autumn so as to tour Scotland to see his relatives and old friends. The winter weather was bad, so he decided to go back to Brazil – he returned the car to John Gates, having done over 40,000 miles in it, with instructions to sell it for him!

It was a 1966 slate-grey saloon – a round-fronted VOLVO 122S saloon. I drove it around the Forest "test circuit". Yes, it would be a very good car for the family, very strongly built and roomy – he reduced the price, acceptable but would Gillian like it – too big, perhaps?

The next day we all went in the Magnette to Brockenhurst. Gill drove the test-drive circuit and returned grinning from ear-to-ear – she loved it!!

We drove home with two strong family cars. Our association with VOLVO had begun.

* * *

One Saturday an elderly man was leaning on our double-gates looking at our Volvo. He lived near Ringwood and was on the committee of the Hants and Dorset Volvo Owners' Club.

I joined the club and during the Day Visit season attended meetings, first at the Mortimer Arms, Ower, then at the Red

Rover at Wellow. Eventually I became Vice-chairman and Treasurer.

We had interesting talks and had an annual Rally at FORT NELSON on Portsdown Hill overlooking Portsmouth. This old anti-Napoleon fort was built facing inland to defend against any French troops trying to take the high ground over Portsmouth!

The Fort was the home to the national collection of Royal Artillery guns: it included a huge 1940s self-propelled caterpillar tracked 75mm artillery gun, on one of which my Canadian cousin, John Gibbons, served in Normandy, the Ardennes and Holland – he was killed by a sniper in the Reichswald in Germany in February 1945.

* * *

Our Volvo 122S model – the twin carburettor model -was solidly built, well rust-proofed underneath, had a stainless steel heavy gauge exhaust system, built like a tank! All these round fronted cars were known as AMAZONS.

Our Amazon served us well for over 100,000 miles, regularly serviced, with no problems.

Several trips to Fishguard in W. Wales for our two-week annual holiday loaded with 3 children, 1 large dog and all our gear. Journeys on to Newport Sands and to Lower Fishguard where we negotiated for a cottage – but didn't buy it – too far from Minstead to supervise and maintain – 260 miles each way.

* * *

One academic year – September to June – our 122S took Gill to Southampton every day – she felt safe even among the heavy transport lorries at "rush hour". She had permission from Hampshire H. Q. to attend a course to qualify for her "P.G.C.E" –

Post Graduate Certificate of Education. Having graduated from Bristol University in 1957 she was due to study for "P.G.C.E" at Salisbury University, Rhodesia in 1968 – but she married me in December 1967 instead! A graduate was, in those days, qualified to teach in schools.

She did her Centre office work at week-ends – I kept an eye on things during the week.

* * *

One Sunday morning I heard the Volvo returning down the lane from Church – it sounded like a tractor! Something seriously amiss! An "expert" friend diagnosed the problem – needed a new crown wheel and pinion, and also a de-coke of the engine with new piston rings. About £700 – too much, I thought so that at 150,000+ miles I traded her in for scrap! A wonderful servant!

A decision I regretted years later when the 122S model was making £6000 on the collector's market!

I ended up buying a later model – a 2 litre engined Amazon. The National Volvo Owners Club booked a "slot" at the Castle Combe Racing Circuit in Wiltshire.

At 6 a.m. Saturday, 15 August 1988 I collected an ally from Calmore, Totton – he had a small workshop where, as a retirement job, he serviced cars, including Volvos – he owned and ran his own Amazon.

We drove my Volvo to Castle Combe Circuit, an old war-time airfield, where we gained access and parked with all the other Volvos.

Other makers of cars were on site as well, all in their own paddocks.

Our Volvo slot on the circuit was just before lunch-time. We had 5 laps allocated. The first, a PARADE lap, when we all processed in line around the circuit – this was so that official and private photographs could be taken.

Castle Coombe Circuit

This done, quite a few Volvos left the circuit and returned to the paddock.

The remainder of us, all clothed in overalls and wearing crash helmets – the stipulated essential kit – then had 4 laps of racing, overtaking and going as fast as we like!

With my friend in the front passenger seat our 4 laps disappeared in no time – another member took photos of us in the "fast corner"!

* * *

Volvo had brought out a square-fronted range – the 144 range, their 244 range with a larger, more powerful engine that became a favourite of the Hampshire Police Force.

An estate car version was produced – one that I had eyed up! Eventually I bought a 2 year old Estate, green in colour.

This estate car gave us sterling service, taking me into retirement.

It took John, plus all his gear backwards and forwards to Queens' College, Cambridge, for 3 years.

It took Jane to and from Birmingham University, Edgebaston, during her 3 year degree course. We always came in from the South-West, trying a variety of routes, including the new Motorway routes!

* * *

I was a "VOLVO MAN "through and through" until my 88th year when I gave my last estate, "945 de lux auto", to John..

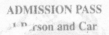

ADMISSION PASS
1 Person and Car

NOTICE
Warning to the public

MOTOR SPORT IS DANGEROUS

Persons attending the track do so entirely at their own risk. It is a condition of admission that Castle Combe Exhibitions Ltd., Haymarket Group Ltd Subsidiary and Associated Companies the landowners and all persons having any connection with the promotion and/or organisation and/or conduct of the meeting (including the drivers and owners of vehicles and passengers in vehicles) are absolved from all responsibility and liability whatsoever arising from negligence, or by accident causing loss, damage or personal injury to spectators or ticket holders, or to their goods or vehicles.

Nº 1495
Castle Combe Circuit
Saturday August 15th 1998

Entrance ticket

Volvos on yard

CHAPTER 24

PROFESSIONAL BODIES

During the early 1970s the Hampshire Environmental Studies Association (H.E.S.A.) had been formed and soon had a membership of over two hundred teachers and their husbands/ wives.

In the winter months we had indoor meetings in schools and colleges. At a meeting in Winchester we had a Cheese and Wine evening with a talk by a "cheese expert": he bought and dealt in cheeses. We learned that the colour, taste and texture of a basic cheddar type cheese varied with the condition of the pasture plants during the seasons. He gave us tasters to make his point.

Eventually we evolved an annual dinner/dance held in January in a school hall in Winchester. Our president, Mr Jeffrey Aldam M.C., Chief Education Officer, always came and joined in. When he retired his successors in turn became President of H.E.S.A.

* * *

One summer Sunday visit was to a sheep farm near Medstead in the Four-Marks area. On retirement the owners had purchased this small farm for the purpose of farming sheep, not for meat but for milk!

They had one huge field, of over 30 acres that sloped gently down to the farm buildings. There was documentary proof that this field had not been tilled for over 1000 years: the pasture consisted of a wide variety of plants native to the area – a very rich food for the sheep.

The sheep, of a strain bred for milk production were machine-milked. We watched the mid-afternoon milking session in the special parlour: hygiene was the order of the day.

A staggered breeding programme ensured that there were always sufficient ewes lactating: some female lambs were hand reared whilst the remainder and the male lambs were sold off for the meat trade.

What did these sheep farmers do with the milk? They made "sheep cheese" and also yogurts!

We all went home with some extremely tasty cheese and a tub of yogurt that my daughter Jane presented to her mother!

* * *

In Minstead two ladies who lived close to Sally's Water Ford kept a flock of goats. These they milked and then produced "Goats' Cheese" that they sold locally. I preferred the Sheep's cheese.

* * *

Over the years we developed out-of-county week-end courses staying in small hotels or hostels from Friday tea-time to Sunday tea-time.

Swanage was a base for studying the Isle of Purbeck, Weymouth for Portland and Chesil Beach and lagoons. Those were "geomorphological" studies, examining rock structures and the associated ecology – the plant and animal life. We were fortunate to have 6th form Grammar School teachers who did the geology side whilst several of us covered the ecology.

Pasture field

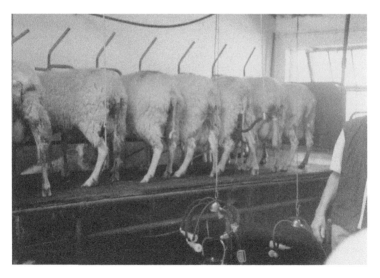

Sheep being milked

* * *

H.E.S.A. was affiliated to the National Association for Environmental Education and our members were able to attend their annual long week-end residential courses that included the A.G.M.

During late August 1979 I took my school boy son John with me to the Annual Conference in Northumberland. It was based at a College of Education at Ponteland, a small town to the North-West of Newcastle. If a lecture did not interest him he could read a book, but of course the long Saturday coach tour was of interest to him: it took in parts of Hadrian's Wall including forts, towers, and settlements.

I, as Chairman of H.E.S.A., was the current Vice-Chair of N.A.E.E., and at the AGM on the Sunday I was elected as Chair of N.A.E.E. I outlined our ideas for the next Annual Conference that would be held in Hampshire at Winchester.

The Conference over, John and I spent five days exploring the northern part of Northumberland and staying in B&B. John adored exploring castles, so we "did" Warkworth, Alnwick, Dunstanburgh, Chillingham, and finally, at low tide over the causeway to Holy Island- Lindisfarne – to Lindisfarne Castle and the Priory – then beating the incoming tide to the mainland. Then southwards to home.

* * *

The committee of H.E.S.A. now had a huge task – the organising of the August 1980 and N.A.E.E. Course Conference.

It would be based at Winchester College of Education (now the University) where there was a large lecture hall and plenty of bedroom accommodation for the expected 150 delegates!

Lectures selected. Then the four contrasting coach journeys for the Saturday showing off different aspects of our county:-

- To the North – Butser Hill, Watership Down, Horse Race country and Kingsclere.
- To the East – the Downs' Valleys – Watercress beds and the Watercress Railway Line, Butser Hill.
- To the South – Portsdown Hill and the Forts, Portsmouth and the Naval Heritage, Gosport and submarines.
- To the Southwest – the New Forest, Lymington and the Solent.

Then we displayed much of the schools' work on Environmental Studies from all parts of the county – all to be collected, mounted and displayed .

Our enlarged committee worked very hard – the result a Winchester Conference that was very successful and remembered by our visitors for a long time.

Next year it would be held in Birmingham.

* * *

I belonged to a professional association – the N.A.H.T – the National Association of Head Teachers.

Employed as a Head Teacher I considered it a sensible move to belong to N.A.H.T for they would always advise on salary and pension rights and on contracts.

Their long established General Secretary was a Barrister-at-Law and was renowned for steering N.A.H.T on a sensible middle of the road approach to educational matters.

I was a member for 24 years, receiving the Quarterly Newsletter. On retirement I became a Life Member and receive an annual newsletter.

* * *

During May 1991 I was fetched from animal feeding to answer the phone – I learned of the death of an old friend of mine in

Staffordshire who had been on the same school staff for several years.

That week I was filling out the 10 yearly Census forms. One question -how many hours had I actually worked that week – 67 hours working, and I remembered that I had put down the same answer 10 years previously!

An article plus graphs from the N.A.H.T came to mind. Heads who worked to 65 years of age, did not, on average live to their 70th birthday. However, those who retired at 60 lived to well over 70 years of age.

I was now in my early 60s, Roy had died aged 69 – it was the right time for me to retire!

For several years I had had two worn out hip joints, but I had soldiered on. I did not consider it fair on the Centre for me to take "sick-leave" to have them done. I would have them replaced once I had retired!

On the Saturday evening I told Gill and the family that I was going to retire at the end of August and that I would be posting my letter giving 4 months notice to Winchester on the Sunday so that they would receive it on the Monday – the last day of May.

I rang Winchester on the Monday morning to make sure that they had received my letter. "But you can't go Stan!" said the senior admin officer. "Sorry, but I am!"

So on the last day of August 1991 we finished moving out of the School House, 24 years after we had moved in!

I left behind a very viable Study Centre plus the field next door to be developed, and a first class Secretary and domestic staff. Wendy, my deputy had retired at the Christmas.

"I shall be living 1 mile away, about 100 ft higher in altitude. I shall not be coming to peep over your shoulder – if there's anything you need to know, the Secretary can ring me." Very best wishes, Stanley"!

CHAPTER 25

ROSE COTTAGE

In 1989 we took the opportunity to buy Rose Cottage. Dating from the late 17th Century it had been a typical "2 up and 2 down" roadside thatched cottage situated on the "well-line" that ran from Castle Malwood hill down to the village.

A deep well was situated close to the back door of the rear of the cottage. There was a large manually-operated pump in the kitchen that had raised water from the well outside.

During the passage of time a lean-to shelter constructed at the rear of the cottage had evolved into a bricked-in felt-roofed structure. About 12 feet deep it spanned the whole width of the cottage – with a rear door in the centre.

When we bought the cottage the single storey lean-to section comprised a kitchen, a bathroom and a bedroom – all squeezed into a 30ft x 10ft space. The felt-roof bowed down in places.

The main roof needed to be re-thatched, the rusty metal frame windows replaced, the interior completely revamped and new electrical wiring installed. An awful lot to be done!

Our architects's proposals for extensions to the cottage to make it into a more modern family home were debated for 18 months with the planning authority: we were refused permission – they were at their strictest at that time. Finally, we exercised our statutory right to build 50 cubic metres of new building in this Conservation area of Minstead.

This provided a single storey extension – a large "farmhouse style" kitchen with two large windows, fitted out with modern kitchen units and a Rayburn stove.

The roof of the original lean-to was raised, cutting into the existing thatch, with the lean-to and kitchen roofed in second-hand Welsh slate.

The old cottage was re-thatched with Turkish wheat straw, new floors upstairs and waterproofed floors downstairs were made. Factory painted window frames with built-in locks replaced the old rusty frames. Re-plastering and decorating throughout and a wood-burning stove fitted in the lounge ingle-nook fireplace – a new home!

* * *

Instead of the mains electricity attached just under the thatch, a special cable brought the mains from a boundary pole under ground to a junction box in the kitchen, with meter boxes outside on the kitchen wall.

Internally all distribution circuits were laid under the upstairs floor boards – there were no electricity wires in the roof space.

* * *

Rose Cottage had about 2 acres of land part of which were attached with the Commoner's Rights. The only one that I have exercised was that of Turberry – allocation of firewood from the neighbouring Crown woodlands.

The land slopes downhill from the cottage to the Forest Fence. The oaks, beeches and hollies on the Forest edge provide shelter from the North and Easterly winds for my bee hives placed near the fence.

The soils of the Rose Cottage 2 acres vary greatly. I am reminded of a Residential Geology Course on the Isle of Wight run by Reading University. The senior lecturer looked over the Solent to the Forest and exclaimed – "The New Forest, an awful geological mess!"

Rose Cottage

Uphill from the cottage the surface loam gives way to a deep layer of white clay. The cottage is built on yellow sand that persists under the front lawn. The meadow and the orchard have a sandy loam structure.

* * *

We demolished the old cess pit to the north of the cottage and replaced it with a family-size Klargester septic tank to take all the cottage waste. The clarified liquid from the Klargester runs in a sealed 4 inch pipe system to the orchard. Here it is distributed to a large soak-away system.

In order to do this we had dug a "porosity" test hole in the orchard: on inspection and testing by an inspector it easily passed the relevant porosity requirement of the Board.

* * *

Rose Cottage, by August 1991, was ready for us to move into.

CHAPTER 26

LATE DAYS
AT THE CENTRE

One Friday tea-time I came home from visiting a school in Farnborough. As I rounded the corner to park by the double gates things looked quite different from normal.

The large female YEW tree near the gates was lying flat across the front lawn with its top branches just touching the dormitory windows! Its roots had peeled back the hedge and hedge-bank for six feet on either side – they were also vertical at the side of the lawn.

A local gale after lunch had caused the yew to keel over. The ground where it had been was now level with the road surface.

What was to be done? I rang up Reg Long to see if he could help.

On the Saturday morning he arrived on his tractor with the trailer full of gear.

With the major part of the tree that was on the lawn cut up and put in piles nearby for disposal our attention was directed to the lower part of the trunk and attached hedge.

I suggested that he saw through the main trunk so that it would be slightly higher than the top of the hedge. This he did.

He attached a metal hauser to the top of the yew trunk and fixed the other end of it to the hook on the back of his tractor that was on the road.

The tractor in gear, a steady pull AND ......

AND – the tree base, the hedge and hedge-bank all fell back into place – within 3 inches of the original position! Sawn off level, the yew became part of the hedge boundary.

An "ill wind" had altered the front appearance of the Centre for ever!

* * *

Late one Friday afternoon John Broomfield, who had been mowing the lawn, came inside to tell me that an elderly man from Australia was leaning on the gates – he had been to school here as a boy.

I invited him to see what alterations I had made to the old village school.

That week I had framed a photograph that I had re-photographed from an original loaned to me by Mrs Sybil White. It showed the top class and their headmaster, Mr Cecil, all dressed up in their "Sunday best". I had placed the photo, plus another of the middle class in their everyday school clothes with their lady teacher, on the top of the lockers in the dining-room.

We came out of the dormitory into the dining room: my elderly visitor went over to the photographs on the lockers, looked at the one with the Headteacher and exclaimed – "Geez, that's me in the front row in my little "sailor suit!" (The two photographs are now displayed in the Green Room, Minstead Village Hall.)

It transpired that the Head and top class had been invited to have tea on the lawn in front of the Manor House in order to celebrate the Coronation of King George V. They had ridden into the Manor on a horse drawn lorry. The Squire's son had joined them for the photo.

My visitor, Billy Iremonger, had been brought up on his father's farm – Robinsbush Farm. His whole school life had been spent at Minstead School.

Yew tree on lawn

Yew being sawn up

Yew – roadside

He and his wife had come over from Australia to visit old haunts: they were going up to Scotland and would be back down in Hampshire during October before sailing back to Sydney.

A quick think. I invited them to have tea with us on the afternoon of the Autumn Open Day.

* * *

At 4pm on the October Open Day, with most of our school visitors gone, I ushered the Iremongers into the Dining room.

To meet them were 3 local ladies who remembered Billy, though were in the middle class at the time.

Also present a reporter plus camera man from the local newspaper. Interviews and photographs over, my elderly guests sat down to a full English cream tea that Gill and her cook had prepared.

Farewells said, I asked Billy if he would let me have his recollections of his schooldays in Minstead. He would.

* * *

EDWARDIAN SCHOOL DAYS
OF BILLY IREMONGER

I started my childhood at Robinsbush Farm, Newtown, Minstead: my father and mother and uncles Charlie and Sam Peckham rented the farm from Squire Compton at the Manor House.

I began school at five years old at the Minstead Council School, 1905, the teachers being Mr Howard Cecil and his wife Mary.

Many of the children those days had to help their parents quite a lot on the small farms that many of them rented. I and other boys near us from an early age had to ride a horse out in the Forest early to find our cows by the sound of their bells, drive them home, then walk quite a distance to school by 9.00am.

Boys dressed mostly in rough corduroy suits, heavy nailed boots, long black stockings for both sexes above the knees, held up by wide black elastic garters, home made. I remember the marks they made, also those cold hard celluloid collars: the girls all wore a clean pinafore every day or else be sent home for one.

Old Ginger Fred Gailor had his family farm and Beer Shop. The locals bought beer there served on a shelf fixed to the outside of the fence, open daily.

Old Fred used to cut my hair sitting on an old chair in the stable just clear of the horse's behind (two pence).

Old Jack Stormes, always with a gun, was the Squire's gamekeeper and lived in a cottage on the hill above Fleetwater ford. His sons could hit almost anything with their catapults or slings which we illegally carried, till we were reported. Then Constable Joyce came to school, took several of us out into the playground, said "Well, are you going to Court or will you take my punishment?" We chose his, then a terrific wallop beside the earhole, a promise to mend our ways, and we lost our weapons till we made new ones.

Anyway our little group of boys had good attendance and fairly good work compared to some. Always work at home with the animals, had to help at times carting ferns, or sedge grass home for litter and turf for the big hearth fire.

We had a big greasy room up the kitchen chimney where we cured bacon for ourselves and others. We had the licensed bull and boar to serve cows and sows in the parish.

We had mixed cattle, usually about forty forest ponies as did others all with common rights.

My father had forty hives of bees till he lost them with Isle of Wight disease prevalent then about 1910. The gypsies used to make the straw hives.

We kept poultry. We had thirty acres so we lost a few wandering fowls to foxes.

The fox hunters no use to us, breaking down hedges and gates, no compensation those days.

Some Fridays I had to go in the big market cart with my eldest uncle Charlie to Millbrook, Shirley and Southampton with butter, eggs, all kinds of apples, vegetables and watercress from our own stream. I had to hold the horse at many stops.

During my early years Lady Harcourt used to give a treat at Christmas at the school in the evening. The magic lantern flickery pictures were not bad and we enjoyed it. Finally each boy and girl had to receive a big brown paper bag containing a few oranges, sweets or cakes, a toy or book according to age. The girls had to curtsey and the boys bow and say "Thank you my lady, God Save the King".

We had much homework at night studying by candlelight or oil lamp.

At school in the morning we hung our caps and bags in the lobby, filed in to our desks, stood and had to say The Lord's Prayer, sat and had an hour of religion, an hour of arithmetic; if fine ten minutes or more in the playground physical drill, English history or geography till 12 meal time for an hour.

Then drawing, tracing on maps, drawing maps from memory, book study of the popular boys stories by good authors, to describe the characters in them later, composition or dictation, the girls doing needlework on some days.

The infants had slates to write on, a box of sand, a coloured bead frame, and strong picture books for the youngest, some four years old. An advanced girl nearly fourteen would teach them.

A little outline of geometry or algebra just before we finished with school, at fourteen.

I think the greatest number of students ever attending was around eighty.

NB. These notes are extracted from a letter sent to the Author by Mr. W. Iremonger from Sydney, Australia in 1979.

* * *

During the long hot August of 1990 two of our children got married, John at Clifton Cathedral, Bristol at the beginning of the month, and Jane at Minstead on an exceedingly hot Saturday at the end of the month.

Sandy, married and living in Gibraltar, came over for Jane's wedding when her two young sons were dressed up as pages.

* * *

August 1991 and news came through to me that my successor at the Centre did not wish to have any animals there.

I consulted the Education Office and was advised to find new homes for all my Centre animals and to give away the poultry houses and arks with them.

My favourites I brought to Rose Cottage. A run with wire netting and netted gate was made in the field immediately below my new garden fence. Their poultry house, on raised bricks, installed, Charles and Petunia the Buff-Back geese came to take up residence with us!

Elgar, my Old English rabbit, came in his ark to live on the large lower lawn.

* * *

The move to Rose Cottage took place at the end of August 1991, using a local removals firm transporting our furniture and effects.

Jock, our young Black Labrador dog was at Rose Cottage with the family. John and his wife, Jane with husband Gareth had come to help us sort out and settle in.

Late afternoon I drove down to the empty School House. For safety reasons I had left our lady cat, Queen Boedica, sitting on a single, small chair in the middle of the lounge, doors and windows locked.

NB Count Ludwig had been put to sleep the year before after both kidneys failed.

I entered the lounge. A forlorn cat greeted me and jumped into my arms.

She and the chair put safely in my car I went back into the house to check through and finally lock up.

Getting into the car I drove away with mixed feelings. We had moved into the house exactly 24 years earlier. It had been my home, and the Centre that I had created – my full-time occupation.

CHAPTER 27

THE EARLY YEARS
OF RETIREMENT

The first few years of retirement were quite eventful.

The layout of the top garden was worked on levelling and grading of lawn surface, planting of flowering trees and shrubs, and the creation of herbaceous and rose borders. Rustic trellis were constructed for climbing and rambling varieties of roses.

The field was mown and a fence with gates was constructed to divide it into two sections. The southern section was laid out as a fruit orchard: in it I planted 24 half-standard apple trees, grouped according to their blossoming period to facilitate cross-pollination during the overall 6 weeks of blossoming.

In the other section of the field my hives of honeybees backed against the forest fence that afforded them some shelter from the North and East winds. The bees did not have to fly far to the orchard to cross-pollinate the apple trees!

* * *

A few weeks after retiring I was visited by our retired doctor, Doctor Danby with a request. The Village Flower Show needed a new treasurer: would I take the position? I did not agree. He called the next week:

On his third visit his persistence paid off – I agreed to become Hon. Treasurer of Minstead Flower Show Society.

The Society was formed after the Second World War in 1951. The annual Flower Show is held on the first Saturday in September in the Village Hall.

There was now plenty of car parking space, for the Village Hall field where we had held fetes had been laid out into marked parking bays: ornamental trees and shrubs had been planted around the edges of the car park.

My first September Flower Show was a very steep learning curve.

Estimating the cash that would be needed, going to Lloyds Bank and returning laden with bags of coins.

Sitting at home making up "floats" for all the side show competitions – eg "guess the weight of the cake", the "bottle tombola", the raffle for the basket of fruit, etc. A float for the entrance desk and a sizeable float for the dining room/kitchen from where afternoon teas would be served during the afternoon once the "notable visitor" had officially declared the Show open!

Then sufficient coins to pay out the Prize Money at the close of the Show – 3 prizes for each of the 90 plus classes.

At the close of the Show as well as paying Prize Money to the queue of winners there was the taking and checking the monies from all the side-shows and competitions.

The Sunday spent checking everything, bagging money to be paid into the Bank the next day and producing a Balance Sheet that would be presented to the Committee in due course.

Phew! A lot of work! But it was a job I enjoyed for seven years as Hon. Treasurer of Minstead Flower Show.

* * *

Within the first 4 years of retirement I had had 2 artificial hip joints at the Southampton General Hospital.

Recovered from these operations I was invited to apply for the post of Parish Clerk. Accepting the invitation I became a paid employee of Minstead Parish Council.

Duties included preparing, in consultation with the Chairman, the agenda for the Council Meetings, the taking and recording of the Minutes of the meetings.

I attended a full-day course for Parish Clerks held at the white Mansion House at Hilliers outside Romsey. This and an approved book that I had bought, proved to be invaluable.

I met on site everyone who had applied for Planning Permission relating to their property, so that I could appraise the Chairman of the situations prior to Council meetings.

The condition of roadways, ditches and roadside trees was inspected regularly. Once a month I would meet an H.C.C. deputy surveyor and in his car we would look at any problems that I, and parishioners, thought needed attention.

The footpaths within the parish had to be inspected regularly so that the paths, stiles, and gateways were in order. A perennial problem was the footpath from Fleetwater to the Church: one section was regularly waterlogged, due to some degree to the soil structure in the field above the path: several, quite expensive solutions to this problem section have been tried over the years!

I resigned as Parish Clerk after 4 years in the job – one that I had enjoyed immensely – but I needed time for other activities.

* * *

On the top Village Green a special memorial tree had been planted to commemorate the Coronation of Queen Elizabeth in 1953.

The tree was a Liquidamber, a N. American sweet gum tree, Liquidamber styraciflua. In autumn the lobed leaves turn from reddish green to a variety of tints – orange, crimson and scarlet.

One day I was walking down to the post-box on the side of the Village Green when I saw a Large White sow and her brood of half-grown pigs. It was the Pannage season when the pigs were allowed to roam looking for beech mast and acorns to eat.

Liquidambar tree

These pigs must have had itchy skin on their backs. To relieve this they were all rubbing their backs vigorously against the large oak circular seat that went round the Liquidambar tree!

I shouted at them and waved my arms but to no avail!

Within minutes the entire seat had been destroyed – just pieces of oak lying on the ground!

At that time I was still Parish Clerk: after conferring with the Chairman we employed Mr Roy Abbott, a F.C. estate carpenter, to build a new oak circular seat around the Liquidambar – BUT with the addition of a strong oak bar just below and behind the front of the seat to prevent pigs from getting their itchy backs under the seat!

Roy's seat is still there today – 2018.

* * *

Pigs at Pannage

In 1995 I was elected a member of Lyndhurst Probus Club. They have an annual knock-out snooker competition, played at the Nondescripts Club in Lyndhurst. I took up snooker and bought myself a cue.

To practise I would walk down to the Social Club at Minstead Village Hall and work on my cueing, etc. on the full size snooker practice table in the large curtained off snooker hall there.

It was now relatively easy, with proposer and seconder, to become a member of the Social Club.

Earlier the large membership had come by car from far and wide, some many miles away. THEN – "Drink Driving" became an offence. Within a year membership had plummeted – locals, like me could now get membership!

CHAPTER 28

THE CHELSEA GOLD MEDAL

After retiring from the Centre my wife Gillian went to Minstead Lodge five mornings a week to help with the work of The Training Project that had been set up there to provide education and skills to young adults with learning disabilities.

The idea had been pioneered at Furzey Gardens using the ornamental gardens and plant nursery as a basis for activities.

The Lodge provided residential accommodation for many students and some members of staff: these students were joined by Day Students for training in horticulture in the 17 acres of grounds and the large Victorian Walled Garden that had old lean-to greenhouses and espalier fruit trees on the walls.

The horticulture section was headed by Peter White. The students learned to cultivate vegetable plots, sow and tend crops to maturity.

In the outbuildings, a large workshop was set up and equipped under the direction of David Robinson, a qualified teacher who taught the correct use of woodworking tools. Students were encouraged and helped to make wooden objects such as bird tables.

Indoors Gillian was in charge of the teaching of Literacy and Numeracy on a one-to-one basis. This was a post that she held and enjoyed for 25 years.

Overall responsibility for the Training Project was Martin

Lenaerts who lived in Seamans Lane. With an "ever-open-door" policy he was always there to listen and advise students with personal problems.

A lot of his "spare" time was spent going around the Forest and neighbouring areas giving talks about the work of The Project, thus gaining donations and grants towards the furtherance of its activities.

Changes were taking place. Students were taken by minibus to Furzey Gardens to work in the propagation unit: here they learned the skills of seed sowing, potting up seedlings, potting-on, etc. They also assisted in the maintenance work in the display gardens. Peter White was in charge of all these activities

Adult "volunteers" were encouraged to give skills to the students – e.g. pottery, art: three hours per week was invaluable. Volunteers also joined staff at Furzey in the shop, refreshment and plant sales and museum areas.

Cuts in external funding from local authorities led to a reduction in the number of residential places and an increase in Day students. Some of the older students had progressed to living in small groups in "out-houses", some under full-time staff supervision: these were situated in the Totton area. They were ferried by minibus from pick-up points in the mornings and returned in the afternoon.

Meantime many of the new Day students had greater personal needs, a few even attending with their carers.

* * *

By early 2010 a meeting of the Furzey Gardens Charitable Trust had decided to apply to the R.H.S. Chelsea Gardens to enter an exhibit in the 2012 Chelsea Flower Show. Chris Beardshaw, a garden designer of national standing and a friend of Furzey, had agreed to design the exhibit.

Chelsea agreed and a site was allocated. It was backing on to a little hillock close to the Thames Embankment entrance.

After consultations and discussions with students and staff, Chris evolved the final design: it would encapsulate the many aspects of Furzey Gardens.

Now the task of producing the hundreds of plants that would be required – the work of the students – proceeded as did the identifying of the larger plants that would have to be transported to Chelsea, and the collection of other materials, e.g. reclaimed timber, undertaken.

Glass rhododendron leaves were designed and produced by Lodge students in their art class.

Finally all to be transported and placed in the Chelsea exhibit. The exhibit to be completed in the comparatively short time allowed on site.

Some staff travelled up daily but Peter White and a core of students lived in a rented house in S.W. London.

After beavering away the exhibit was completed by the Sunday evening! The gardens "acid woodland edge" was topped by our Master Thatcher's Lantern Building: Simon Sinkinson crafted it from fallen spiny oak boughs and straw thatch. The anti-clockwise stairs led to a high open apex that allowed light to flood down on to the glass rhododendron leaves.

During the Monday Royal walk-about the Queen spent some time looking at the exhibit and speaking to the designer and team members including one student, SIMON BOURNE. She took on board that the exhibit was a celebration of the talents and abilities of people with learning disabilities.

NB. Several years later, whilst touring the New Forest Show at Brockenhurst, the Queen stopped and went into the roadside Furzey/Lodge exhibit that was staffed by staff and students. With no prompting the Queen spoke to Simon Bourne and said – "How good to see you again Simon!" What a memory!

The Tuesday morning, when the judges' awards were announced, Gill went into the office at the Lodge at 8.50am. All were agog. What would we get? Then the phone rang – An RHS GOLD MEDAL for the exhibit! Gill rang me – wonderful news.

* * *

As an R.H.S. Member I had got tickets for the Wednesday afternoon/evening period, two for us and two for friends who drove us up to Chelsea. Entering through the Thames Embankment turnstile we were close to the Furzey Exhibit. Simon Sinkinson, our Master Thatcher, was on duty and to the surprise of onlookers invited us through the exhibit gate and into the Lantern building. Up the stairs into the open apex from where we waved to the people below!

Then we toured the Showground. Evening, and no crush to go round the vast tented marquee and looked at the exhibits at close quarters. Home late in the evening – a visit to remember!

The Chelsea show ended on the Saturday and then the hard work started again for the Minstead team. The whole exhibit – lock, stock and barrel – was dismantled and, every plant included, transported back to Furzey within the time scale allowed by the R.H.S. The site had to be left in the condition in which we had found it!

* * *

Fast forward. The Gold Medal winning Chelsea exhibit had been reconstructed in a lowland bog area of Furzey Gardens just above the lake.

We went to the opening ceremony. Chris Beardshaw told me that he had not had the opportunity to study any horticulture at school. The subject "Rural Studies" (that I had been the Chief

Examiner for in the mid 1960s) had been dropped from school curricula in favour of more time for academic subjects.

And now, in 2018, the pendulum is swinging back again, as it does over the years in education! Rural Studies under different names are coming back into favour!

CHAPTER 29

THE VILLAGE HALL

The Village Hall has been the base for many village activities. The Dramatic Society has regularly put on plays under many directors – David Balfour, Chris Ware, Sandy Aylen and Geoff Green to mention a few.

Attending the Doctor's Surgery at the end of the hall was sometimes risky. "Stanley, I have a small part for you in the next play – you will take it?" Thus I became the "first ghostly sailor" who spoke first at the start of "Under Milk Wood"!

In Geoff Green's production of "Lark Rise to Candleford" I had the minor role of a villager, Old Dick. Near the end of the play the village women gathered and declared that they knew when the menfolk would be leaving the pub – just after Old Dick had sung his song!

The song about an Evil Knight who took maidens plus their horses and belongings from their homes during the night had many verses ending with the last maiden throwing the evil knight to his death in the sea!

I spent many late evening hours learning the song that I sang in a "rural voice".

Before the play started, Marion Young, the pianist said – "You only need to sing two verses, Stanley!" – I replied "I have learned it and I will sing the lot"!

So, towards the end, Old Dick walked to the edge of the stage and sang the whole song gesturing to the audience to join in the chorus lines of each verse! This they did and enjoyed it – so did I!

My wife, Gillian, has been an excellent actress and has taken roles in many Minstead productions, notably a lead part in "The Chalk Garden". Chris Ware produced a "play in the round" where "set" was in the centre of the main hall with the audience seated around it: Gill's part included going around the set with a vacuum cleaner exclaiming "Hoover, Hoover, – Hoover Hoover"!

Drama society productions continue to the present day, as does the young peoples' pantomime that was pioneered many years ago by Nick Mellersh and Junior Minstead.

* * *

On several Sundays in each year this century the Village Hall has been host to ANTIQUE FAIRS. Stall holders would start arriving soon after 7a.m. in order to set up their stalls or tables in the main hall. Coming from far and wide, including Bournemouth, their goods for sale included jewellery, china and pottery, glassware, artwork, books, postcards, and philately, etc.

The organisers advertised widely, placing wooden roadside signs at main road junctions, leading to the village, and many signs in the village directing visitors to the Hall: sometimes the event was advertised as a "Flea Market".

The Autumn often saw a Toy Fair and sometimes a "Model Railway" day when large working layouts of both "0.0" and "0.0.0" gauge railways were set up. Collectors' items of rolling stock were on sale.

Always one paid an entrance fee to enter the hall. Refreshments were often available.

Closing at tea-time, the hall was emptied and cleaned up by early evening when the last cars and vans would drive post Rose Cottage on their way to the A31 road.

This was yet another source of revenue for the Village Hall.

* * *

For many years there has been an Auction Sale at the Village Hall on a Monday evening. During the day many people, including dealers, arrive with items they wish to sell. The items are placed on the rows of tables extending down the length of the hall. Large items are placed on the floor near the entrance doors.

I have attended the auction on two occasions paying a small entrance fee at the door. The auctioneers proceed at speed along the tables of items for sale, there being a minimum bid. Few lots exceeded the ten pound mark.

The biggest item that I saw at the auction was a petrol-driven roller lawn mower, parked on the floor near the entrance doors.

Buyers had to go to a desk where they paid for their purchase: a commission fee had been included. Likewise the sellers had to pay a commission fee deducted from their proceeds.

At the close of the auction everything had to be packed away so that the hall was left in the condition that they found it on the Monday morning.

I understand that the auctioneers hold several auctions a week in different halls in the area.

The fee for the weekly auction makes a valuable contribution to the costs of maintaining the Village Hall.

Early this century we enjoyed several "dinner dances" held at the Hall. Groups of people sat at squares of tables down one side of the hall where they had a meal and also imbibed liquid refreshments bought from the Social Club bar extension in what is now the Green Room. Between times we danced on the floor – like old times. These events were held to raise money for charities.

* * *

In costume

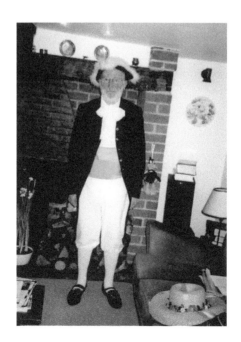

Dom and Gill

Trafalgar dinner

A very special event was held in the hall to celebrate the 200th anniversary of the Battle of Trafalgar that took place on 21st October 1805.

It was organised by Dom Young, a one-time Royal Naval commander in charge of the engineering department of one of our nuclear submarines.

There were two provisos for attending this event that included a sit-down meal:-

1. we had to go dressed in period costumes appropriate to 1805
2. we would make a sizeable donation to the R.N.L.I. for which Dom became an area representative.

Yes! The relevant costume hiring companies did a roaring trade.

Appended are my photographs of Gillian and me "in costume", of Gillian with Dom, and of the scene looking down the long table.

We all enjoyed a wonderful evening, and a considerable sum was raised for the R.N.L.I.

* * *

The local medical practice ceased using the end room of the hall as a surgery many years ago. Patients have to travel to the surgery at the top of Church Lane in Lyndhurst.

The room is often used as a dressing room for actors in Dramatic Society plays.

* * *

The Green Room, now known as the Danby Room, is used for meetings including the regular meetings of the Minstead Parish Council.

* * *

The Social Club hosts the meetings of the Local History Group.

Wednesday evenings have become a Motor Cycle meeting place: experienced riders on a wide variety of machines come from far and wide to enjoy a social evening. It is interesting for me as a one-time motorcyclist, to listen to the different exhaust notes as they ride past us during the late evening on their way to the A31 at the top of our hill.

CHAPTER 30

UP AND AWAY!

On the 1st January 2001 our son John took the overnight flight from Heathrow to Cape Town. He had a 2 month contract to conduct opera at the Spier International Opera Festival on the edge of the Winelands North of Cape Town. He had been provided with a car and a furnished flat in an apartment block at Sea Point, a seaside suburb of Cape Town.

From there he rang me. "From the front window I can see the giant Lion Head Rock. From the rear window is a long low hill." "Yes, John, that long hill is Signal Hill from which the NOON DAY GUN is fired – I know where you are within a few hundred yards!"

I was recovering from a severe bout of arthritis. Seeing my doctor, David Balfour, I asked whether I was fit to fly to Cape Town. "Yes, go Stan, go – it will do you good!"

So a week later Gillian and I took the overnight Virgin Atlantic flight from Heathrow to Cape Town. We were met by John and stayed at his flat. Outside the block, on the roadside wall was a notice to say that it was guarded by an "armed response" organisation 24 hours a day. If there was any intruder problem observed from the flat we were to dial the "armed response" number: they would be there within minutes!

Driving to the city we were to keep the car doors locked and windows closed when stopping at traffic lights or junctions – thus was the security situation!

The city had changed a lot since we had sailed home from there in 1960! Much new building but the main features remained. We visited the Cathedral and walked through "The Gardens", past the SMUTS statue to gaze at Table Mountain in the distance.

On days when John was rehearsing at Spier, I would have my usual post-breakfast walk along the promenade opposite and gaze at the waters of Table Bay. Then we would catch a service bus into the city where we explored the Dock Side development with its many shops and restaurants on 2 floors. Stunning views over the dock area and of course the huge Table Mountain dominating the view: sometimes it wore its "table-cloth" when the entire summit was covered with clouds.

When John was free we drove north to the winelands around Paarl and Stellenbosch. We walked through the large Kirstenboch Gardens below the inland side of Table Mountain.

One morning we drove to the Lower Cable Station and took the cable car to the Upper Cable Station on the top of the mountain. It was a clear day. We walked the whole length of Table Mountain to glimpse Devils Peak further along, and then walked back again, savouring the wonderful views from this 3,563ft high mountain that I had first glimpsed as a dot on the horizon 400 miles away from the deck of my Dutch liner in 1957. We eventually docked under it in Duncan Dock – my introduction to South Africa.

Our final evening. A production of La Boheme. We looked across the open-air auditorium, John conducting the actors singing on stage with a large African moon rising above the stage.

A moment to remember – for ever!

* * *

Flight home the next day. A take-off towards dusk when the air has cooled and will provide more "lift" for the aircraft. The overnight flight is over the ocean, keeping well away from any land-based conflicts. Over land again to the north of the Gulf of Guinea, thence to reach the Mediterranean over Tunisia.

It makes us realize how vast is the continent of Africa – over five-sixths of our flying time has been over Africa!

Crossing the N. W. tip of Spain, to France, then an early landing at Heathrow – an uneventful flight of almost 12 hours duration.

* * *

During the next 10 years we took many overseas holidays. To cope with my sensitivity to U.V.A. and U.V.B radiation I used prescribed sun barriers on my skin, had my shirt collar turned up, and wore my large light brown broad-brimmed hat – not an Aussie bush hat, but a woollen hat purchased from John Lewis in Southampton!

This hat was squashed in many overhead aircraft lockers but always came back to shape when worn. It became known as "Ma-hat-ma" and may feature in a children's book in the future.

* * *

Spain we visited on 4 tours. Madrid and its Art Galleries, by super fast train to Cordoba where we entered the vast Mosque inside which the Catholics had built a full size Cathedral!

Granada with the long main avenue that led downhill to our hotel: it was lined with Judas trees that were in full flower. Two visits to the Alhambra to marvel at the gardens and the architecture.

Finally to the Rioja region, thence following the "Pilgrims Way" through Gallicia via Leon's cathedral to Santiago de Compostella staying in Parador hotels all the way, the one at Santiago having been the hospital built for the pilgrims. Crammed just inside the West door of the Cathedral we witnessed the lighting of the incense in the giant testa, that was then swung by ropes, high above the chancel, until the monks had it swinging to an almost horizontal position by the East and West doors, so that we could see the burning incense inside it, as the organ played. Our final evening – in the moonlight – we sat on a bench outside our Parador looking across the empty square whilst several squares away a musician played melodies on a saxophone: above the cathedral of St James a solitary light shone, the "beacon light" to guide the pilgrims.

* * *

East Africa on five visits on one of which we had a dawn flight in a hot-air balloon over the Masai Mari, saw the sun-rise three times, watched elephants waking up, and other animals stirring on the near treeless landscape. A bumpy landing after 45 minutes at a prescribed spot where the waiting ground crew conveyed us to sit at tables for a full champagne breakfast!

A journey through Tanzania in a Toyota Land Cruiser with two other persons and our driver/guide who had, for 20 years been the senior veterinary officer for the Serengeti – why change? Far more money taking tourists around! He was able to drive our vehicle down the steep track (half a mile below) to the floor of the vast NGORONGORO CRATER.

This perfect caldera, 10 miles across, is the largest in the world.

At least 3 distinct climatic zones and a large Soda Lake: most wild animals were to be found living there with the exception of giraffes.

We ended up driving to the great Serengeti Plain to live for 4 nights in a large, custom built tent close to a ravine where a hippo spent the day. Lions roamed around at night and we had armed guards to take us to and from the dining tent where we had a 4 course dinner every evening! A team of 5 caring for the 4

Vet – guide and me – Serengeti

Our tent – Serengeti

of us plus our guide. It would all be packed away and taken away on the lorry within 24 hours of us leaving – the site to be left as they had found it!

A flight to Zanzibar – "the spice islands" where we stayed for 4 days in a hotel in the "old town" – dinner at night gazing through the open window over the beach to the Indian Ocean.

Day trips through the island discovering the flora and the many spices produced there: A flight to Nairobi, to catch the night flight to London.

* * *

A flight from Vienna with Austrian Airlines to Beijing in China after a dawn crossing of the vast Gobi Desert. Our tour included a 5 day cruise up the Yangste River, through a lock in the nearly completed Hydro-electric dam to sail through the "3 Gorges" whose cliffs towered above the river – so narrow in the Gorges that one-way traffic was enforced with huge semaphore type signals at either end: a queue of ships were waiting at the far end as we exited the gorges. Our ship voyage ended at Chongqing from where we flew to Xian, the ancient capital of China whose old city walls were high and very wide. Nearby was the roofed-over site of the Terracotta Warriors – all had different expressions on their faces!

To the Great Wall, where we walked in a section, opposite to the section walked by visiting dignities!

From our 14-storey hotel bedroom window, several miles from Beijing city centre, we watched morning "rush hour". Two 6 lane highways crossed each other with a large Clover-leaf junction not far from us. Queueing were cyclists by the thousand, cars by the hundred and many buses of all types – articulated, double decker, coaches, etc. A large city with a huge population on the move.

Tiananmen Square: a section was being cleaned: the squad of convicts had scraped off the chewing gum deposits and now a fleet of lorries were following each other round and round with their scrubbing brushes cleaning the surface

Surrounding the square, many buildings including a museum and the huge "parliament" building. People were selling "Beijing Olympic 2008" caps advertising the forthcoming Olympic Games 2008 so, of course, we bought two to add to our souvenirs.

We flew from Beijing airport with memories of many places in this huge nation: we had learned a lot about its long and fascinating history. Now, a nation on the march!

Our airliner encountered strong headwinds over the Ural Mountains, slowing us so that we missed the connecting flight from Vienna to London and had to wait three hours for the next one.

* * *

Southern Africa called. Tours that included visits to Pretoria and the Voortrekker Monument, Wildlife spotting in the Kruger National Park, Swaziland, Port Elizabeth, the Little Karoo, Worcester – Vineyards and brandy distillery, then to the Paarl and Stellenbosch Vineyards.

To celebrate our Golden Wedding in 2007, St. Cuthbert's Church, Gweru, Zimbabwe was out of the question. We flew via Johannesburg to Port Elizabeth and a leisurely 7 day tour to Cape Town where we spent four lazy days under Table Mountain. Taking off with South African Airways for Heathrow, I left a part of me in my favourite city!

* * *

A flight to Los Angeles from where we joined the American Trafalgar Tour Company to ride in a large coach on a 14 day tour: most passengers were from the East Coast – they wanted

Cape Town from across Bay

Cape Town – docks development

to discover the West of their country! Many lengthy drives between sites of interest.

Phoenix, thence to the Grand Canyon: a helicopter had crashed into it the day before, so no one on the coach wished to go up today – except the two Gibbonses (it won't happen 2 days running!). We were weighed and allocated our seats in the helicopter (it had to be balanced). Then we took off for a 1 hour 40 minute flight over the canyon, 12 miles to the North Rim, then back observing the Colerado River flowing thousands of feet below us: many photographs taken – the risk had been worth taking!

Las Vegas – amazing. Bryce Canyon with its many coloured rock formations, to the Yosemeti National Park with its sheer massive El Capitan and bears in its woodland habitats. The drive through the Sierras with the vast Almond orchards in the lower reaches before arriving in San Francisco. A cruise in the bay to under the Golden Gates, then one day, after 4pm we took lifts to go to the Observation Lounge at the top of the Bank of America, by far the tallest building in the city. From the all-round windows we looked down upon the whole city and Golden Gates in the distance.

The coach tour finished with a leisurely drive down the coastal road to Los Angeles. The famous wide pavement in which are the memorial slabs was carefully inspected, then round the corner to glimpse on the distant hillside the large white letters that spelt out HOLLYWOOD!

As the BRIT on the coach, I gave the Vote of Thanks to our driver, to our very informative and caring young "Confederate" Southerner courier/guide and to the many new friends that we had met on the journey through the vast and captivating country. I ended with "GOD BLESS AMERICA!"

* * *

An overnight direct flight from Heathrow took us to Windhoek, the capital of NAMIBIA, once German S. W. Africa. This vast country borders the Kalahari Desert: much of the land is desert or semi-desert with the northern section of its South Atlantic coast known as The Skeleton Coast.

We were told that the land area was a big as Austria and that the population of over one and a quarter million was divided between the northern belt bordering Angola and the area around Windhoek.

The German army was defeated by South African forces in 1915 and the territory became a South African protectorate. They ruled it until Namibia gained independence. Many of the main roads on which we travelled were dead straight for many miles with no vegetation within 50 yards of either side: they were so built in order that Air Force planes could use them as runways!

We were taken to see The Bottomless Lake into which the defeated German army deposited their heavy weapons, including their artillery guns.

Northwards through Game Reserves and semi-desert farming country with the roadside dwarf cacti surviving the attentions of the large grading machines that maintained the surface of these dirt roads.

In the North-west corner, near the Angolan border, we made a dawn visit to an observation point on the edge of a huge dried-up salt lake stretching in all directions as far as the eye could see. As our guide remarked – "from here you can discern the "Curvature of the Earth!" Our guide, a tall South African qualified teacher had come with his family to Namibia on its independence: they had taken up Namibian citizenship – his wife teaching in a Windhoek High School, whilst he enjoyed his life as a tourist guide.

In the desert areas we would see some small clumps of shrubs and small trees where underground streams watered their roots.

Namibia – dried salt lake

Sand dunes – dawn Sousesvlei

To a hilly area where we spent two nights in a hotel complex with individual chalets perched between the huge rocks.

Thence to the coast and the port of Walvis Bay that serviced Oil Drilling Rigs, some of which were anchored off shore.

In this area was a large chalet and bungalow township complex close to the sandy Atlantic shore – these were owned by Germans who flew in with Lufthansa, 6 flights a week during the long holiday season.

South to an isolated hotel complex – the nearest building 12 miles away. We walked from the lounge, dining room complex about 40 yards to our all mod cons chalet.

After dinner on the first evening our guide took us away from the hotel, all external lights off, to look up at the Southern Sky. At our high altitude and through the clean air we gazed at the myriads of stars. Wow!

The next morning, a pre-dawn start, driving many miles to Sousesvlei to see the rising sun illuminate the vast sand dunes that stretched into the distance on either side of the dirt track.

Back to Windhoek – to walk in the streets comparing the old German architecture with the very modern multi-storey office and residential block.

A country with good potential for its future. Uranium mines in the north worked by an Australian firm: huge deposits of Diamonds to the South worked by a South African firm in an area debarred to tourists – you could pick up handfuls by the sea shore! In both the Uranium and Diamond firms the Namibian Government controlled 51 per cent of the shares.

We flew home with many memories of this vibrant young nation.

Our final long overseas tour!

CHAPTER 31

AND FINALLY

In 1967 The Honeysuckle Tea Rooms was a long established business drawing many customers from far and wide: with its spacious off-road parking it was a focal point for a leisurely visit to Minstead and the neighbouring forest area.

The business was eventually bought by Frank and Mary Adcock. The large thatch-roofed building had dining rooms, with kitchen and preparation rooms downstairs: upstairs was living accommodation. It was developed as a bespoke evening dinner restaurant, a favourite haunt of the manager and first-team players of Southampton Football Club.

We watched as a huge mobile crane on the road lifted the two pre-fab. buildings from a lorry overhead to lower them on prepared bases on the far garden end of the property! These joined up buildings formed the Honeysuckle Tea Rooms that served morning coffee, light lunches and teas.

The Adcocks sold the business properties and retired to a house in Burley.

The new owners continued trading, but one day an accident happened! After lunch we heard and saw a succession of fire engines racing down past Rose Cottage.

The Honeysuckle was ablaze, the thatch roof then the whole building. By the next morning only the shell of walls remained!

Eventually the ruins were removed and the site levelled. Now it is a large empty site, gently sloping to the tiny stream at the rear, and covered with "natural vegetation". It is fenced securely to keep out animals and humans!

Thus, a large empty plot exists near the centre of the village.

* * *

Gusts from a strong Easterly gale flattened a section of my climbing roses support by the main garden pathway and by dawn we could see that it had damaged the Liquidamber tree on the Green. A large side branch had been broken off and several other branches damaged.

What was to be done? Under the direction of ex-Head Forester Geoff Green broken pieces were removed and the tree re-shaped.

Now, several years later the tree appears in tip-top condition and ready to sport its amber and crimson September leaves.

* * *

The old mature oak and beech trees opposite us were next to cause concern.

One oak was dying back: some branches were in danger of breaking off and falling on to the road. Permission was given by the Council for the top half to be cut down. With the help of a "cherry picker" and free-climbing woodmen we witnessed the work take place.

A few years later, Xmas-time, a northerly gale caused another oak, almost opposite our front garden, to be partially uprooted and lean at 45 degrees against the next door oak! A two-day job by a climbing woodman to take it down and cut damaged sections off the oak on to which it was leaning!

The huge base and root-section was hoisted by crane on to a large lorry to be taken away.

The result of all this – more afternoon light on to our front garden!

View downhill from Rose Cottages

* * *

By 2001 the upper end of Church Lane had changed.

Since the retirement of the Rev Delaney the red-brick Rectory had been empty. It was sold by the Church Authorities to a private buyer.

Opposite the "old" rectory a development of housing, Church Close, was built by a Housing Association. Accessed over a cattle grid there is parking space by the properties. A large lawned area leads to a tall roadside screen of trees. The development was intended for use by Minstead residents in need of housing.

* * *

In the church an appeal had raised the money to purchase another Bell – the six bells would give a much larger number of peals. There is now a large group of keen campanologists from Minstead and the surrounding neighbourhood.

* * *

On the Remembrance Sunday, the names of : "THE FALLEN" are read out during the morning service at the end of which the visiting priest and congregation process down Church Lane to the War Memorial where the poppy wreath is laid by the Chairman of the Parish Council. This is followed by prayers and

"At the going down of the sun, and in the morning, we will remember them" – "WE WILL REMEMBER THEM!"

Of recent years, the area branch of the British Legion has held a service by the War Memorial on the Saturday.

This year, 2018, the British Legion invited the public to take part in a movement to say "Thank you" to the First World War generation who died in that war that ended 100 years ago. They have offered for sale metal near-life-size silhouettes. The Parish

Council has asked for donations to purchase a silhouette – a "Classic Tommy" that will be attached to a wooden post close to the War Memorial.

* * *

Some years ago the Trusty Servant was refurbished, the original car parking area at the front now levelled and surrounded by a brick wall. Upstairs the bedroom area was transformed into high-spec suites.

During the winter months they have provided monthly Village Lunches in the dining area. Choose one main course from four offered, at a very competitive special price: order and pay at the bar, then wait at a table next to village friends. A few minutes later your large plate is brought through from the kitchen where the dish has been freshly prepared by the chef. The monthly Village Lunch has proved to be very popular.

* * *

Sadly the Village Shop with its café has been permanently closed by the owners.

Now a trek to a neighbouring village in order to buy newspapers and provisions and to visit a Post Office.

Times have changed!

* * *

Time has been called on a major hobby of mine – Beekeeping, that I began over 60 years ago. Last year I gave my last two hives of bees to ex-students.

I served as chairman of the New Forest association for 33 years, as chairman of the Hampshire Federation for 6 years then as their President.

I taught and tutored the craft for many years. I have been left with many happy memories, many of which will feature in the book that I am about to start to write –

"TO BE OR NOT TO BEE!"

* * *

We are now part of the New Forest National Park that spans an area much larger than the New Forest District Council Area. The local week-end paper prints two sets of Planning Applications – one for the N.F.D.C., the other for the National Park Authority. Any Minstead applications – to alter or extend properties, to add out-buildings, etc – are adjudicated upon by the New Forest National Park Authority, Lyndhurst, after receiving comments and recommendations from the Parish Council.

Today a journey from the A31 cattle grid through the entire village area shows many "new" or extended houses of which many would be valued at £1 million – a further evolution of Minstead.

* * *

It is September 2018. At nearly 90 years of age and, recovering from knee and shin-bone surgery, I am completing the writing of this book.

Over the years I have become a part of the Village and neighbouring Forest area.

I have watched it evolve.

IT IS MY HOME
"MINSTEAD – 50 YEARS AND COUNTING!"

Author 2018

STANLEY GIBBONS
Thinking of those on the far distant shore.

APPENDICES

APPENDIX 1

MARKER 7

From Anses Wood Nature Trail

This small evergreen bushy plant is called

<u>BUTCHER'S BROOM</u>

DO NOT PICK PIECES OFF IT

The leaves that you see are not really leaves but are really side stems doing the work of leaves!

Carefully feel the pointed tip of a leaf with your finger.

<u>BUTCHER'S BROOM</u>

How long is a "leaf"? .... cm.

In early summer tiny white flowers appear on the middle vein of the "leaves". Tiny green berries develop from the flowers: they turn red when ripe.

<u>AT SCHOOL</u> Find out why these plants are called BUTCHER'S BROOM

APPENDIX 2

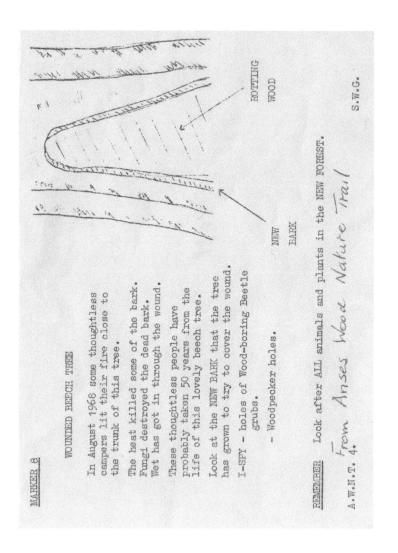

MARKER 8

WOUNDED BEECH TREE

In August 1968 some thoughtless
campers lit their fire close to
the trunk of this tree.

The heat killed some of the bark.
Fungi destroyed the dead bark.
Wet has got in through the wound.

These thoughtless people have
probably taken 50 years from the
life of this lovely beech tree.

Look at the NEW BARK that the tree
has grown to try to cover the wound.

I-SPY – holes of Wood-boring Beetle
grubs.

– Woodpecker holes.

REMEMBER   Look after ALL animals and plants in the NEW FOREST.

From Anses Wood Nature Trail

A.W.N.T. 4.

ROTTING WOOD

NEW BARK

S.W.G.

APPENDIX 3

<u>LET THE BELLS RING!</u>

****

<u>A L L   S A I N T S   C H U R C H,   M I N S T E A D</u>

CHURCH BELLS APPEAL

Our church has been the constant factor in Minstead life for over 700 years. Generation after generation of Minstead people have been baptised, confirmed, married therein - and finally they have been laid to rest in the beauty and peace of the churchyard.

Today, as we celebrate the 700th anniversary of Robert, the first recorded rector, Minstead Church is still very much alive and vibrant as it continues to carry its essential message of Christianity to us in the late 20th Century.

The three church bells, dating from 15th Century to 1638 A.D. are now in need of repair and re-hanging. The March A.G.M. of the Church endorsed the decision of the elected Parochial Church Council to proceed with the work to the existing bells and, as the opportunity has arisen, of having two smaller bells cast and tuned with the existing three to make a "peal of five". We now have twenty persons of all ages learning bellringing from a member of the Guild of Ringers and they are looking forward to being able to ring the one hundred and twenty "changes" possible from the "peal of five" instead of the six "changes" from the present "peal of three".

Minstead is far from being a wealthy church: in fact we rely upon the tourist season for our continuing solvency. Our decision to proceed with the bell project must be seen as a symbol of our faith in the future of our church in this materialistic age.

We invite all who live within the sound of Minstead church bells, as well as those further afield, to support our project by making a donation towards the cost of the work.

OUR TARGET IS £5000

For all donations large or small - THANK YOU
(Cheques payable to "Minstead Parochial Church Council")

****

LET THE BELLS RING!

****

The Parochial Church Council,
All Saints Church,
Minstead.

APPENDIX 4

Activity	CHURCH FETE Receipts on 26th May		Additional sales	
Bookstall	41	03		
Bottle stall	106	95 *		
Cake stall	48	63		
Craft stall	71	77	6	00
Plants stall	70	26	1	00
Produce stall	38	49		
Raffles	36	62 *	9	90
White Elephant	105	54		
Admissions	50	74		
Refreshments	90	75 *		
Trade /craft stalls	28	59		
Auction	11	00		
Side shows :-				
Balls in bucket	7	00		
Bossing thro' target	9	07		
Darts	5	45		
Floating Plate	9	30		
Golf	8	20		
Pony Rides	5	50		
Roll-a-coin	4	57		
Roulette wheel	2.1	71 *		
Soft drinks	12	00		
Stocks	2	20		
	£815 – 37			

NB. after deduction
of "floats"

* indicates that this
total has not had the
stall expenses deducted
from it.

APPENDIX 5

MINSTEAD CHURCH FETE   26TH MAY 1980

RECEIPTS			EXPENSES		
Receipts at Fete	815	37	Insurance	47	50
Pre-fete raffle receipts	9	90	Advertising	8	90
Donations	7	00	Draw tickets	4	50
Subsequent receipts :-			Prizes	18	30
Surplus cider – 5 cases	31	20	Minstead Hall fee	10	00
" bottles	4	10	Refreshments; prizes;		
Knitwear	6	00	cider; bottles	83	36
Plants	1	00	Shop – soft drinks	6	27
	974	57	Boys' Brigade Band	15	00
	125	68	Adaptor plug replacement	1	25
Profit	678	89		195	69

[signature] Hon. Treasurer, P.C.C.

[signature]

259

APPENDIX 6

Please accept and return to
Hon. Treasurer &

W. A. HUGHES
DOUGLAS HUGHES
ALAN HUGHES

TELEPHONE Nº
01-247 2599

S. W. GIBBONS
MINSTEAD RURAL STUDIES
CENTRE,
MINSTEAD, LYNDHURST,
HAMPSHIRE SO4 7GJ
CADNAM (042 127) 3437

Whitechapel Bell Foundry Ltd.

(A.D. 1570)

The Parochial Church Council,
The Parish Church,
Minstead,

32 & 34. Whitechapel Road,

London. E.1.

To the order of:-

Mr. Michael Clarke,
Greenbrae,
Minstead,
Lyndhurst,
Hants.
SO4 7FX

Invoice No.312/80.

28th April,1980.

CB/49/79.	Minstead Parish Church bells.		
To:	Dismantling the three bells and sending with the wheels to the Foundry. Oiling and tightening frame bolts and painting. Cutting out the cast-in clapper staples and drilling centre holes. Tuning the three bells to the major scale. Providing new fittings for the bells, consisting of:-		
	Cast iron headstocks and ball bearings mounted on steel bearing plates. Insulation pads and supporting bolts. Clappers and clapper staples. Stays, sliders, runner boards and slider pins. Nylon ball bearing pulleys and bell ropes.		
	Adapting and fitting new rims to the wheels. Preparing and painting all iron and steel and impregnating timber with Solignum. Turning the bells and "stocking down. Delivering the bells and fittings to the Church and hoisting into the tower. Fitting the bearings to the bell frame; fitting up and hanging the bells and leaving all ready for use.	£3,162	00
	Extra for casting a resin pad on the inside and outside of the crown on the treble.	47	50
	Casting two smaller bells to augment the peal to five; 2'4" and 2'2" in diameter, weighing ∅ 4-0-13 and ∅ 3-2-1 respectively, and accurately tuning them to agree with the existing bells. Providing complete ringing fittings as enumerated above.		
		£3,209	50	C/Fwd.

V.A.T. REGISTRATION NO
172 1372 24

APPENDIX 7

Invoice No.312/80 Contd/.

Minstead Parish Church bells.

B/Fwd.	£3,209-50
Delivering, fitting up and hanging and leaving all ready for use. Including Bellhangers' time, assistance, expenses and cartage etc.	£3,383-00
Casting inscriptions on the two bells, 36 letters @ 40 pence per letter.	14-40
	£6,606-90

Less allowance for local assistance provided,	622-00	
and a further allowance for dismantling the three bells and all cartage.	217-00	839-00
		£5,767-90

By credit in respect of two old bells provided:-

16" diameter	1-0- 2	
11¼" "	1-11	
Ø 1-1-13 @ £126 per cwt.		172-12
		£5,595-78

Allowance in respect of board and lodgings provided for our Bellhanger.	75-00
	£5,520-78
VAT @ 15%	828-12
	£6,348-90

Received with thanks. 4th June,1980.
p.p. WHITECHAPEL BELL FOUNDRY LTD.

APPENDIX 8

MINSTEAD CHURCH BELL APPEAL

RECEIPTS		EXPENDITURE

PRIVATE DONATIONS – Named,
Anon., Casual Visitors ... £ p 3216·36

Whitechapel Bell
Foundry £6368·90

GRANTS

Barron Bell Trust £500
W'chester + Plmouth Guild
of Church Bellringers £400
Compton Legacy £1500
Harcourt Legacy £291·78
Furzey Gardens Charitable
Trust £400
Minstead Carnival £200
Junior Minstead £40 .... 3331·78

EVENTS + DONATIONS

Church Fete profit £678·89
Maypole Dancing £38·43
Midsummer Madness £101·97
Music in the Church £94·40
Harvest Supper profit £10
Youth Carol Singers £51
Bell Ringers £53
Dedication Service coll. £41·38 .... 1069·57

BANK INTEREST on deposits. 543·28

TOTAL RECEIPTS £8160·89

NB.
BALANCE IN HAND OF
RECEIPTS OVER
EXPENDITURE WAS
£1811·99 on
23rd December 1980.
Account closed on
this date and balance
dispersed as follows
with P.C.C. approval :-
£1000 to Fabric Fund
£811·99 to Church Bank
Dep. a/c.

A. Gibbons
HON. TREASURER
P.C.C.

D.M. Davies

APPENDIX 9

Minstead

6 June 1988

Dear

Sunday 5th June 1988 will be a never to be forgotten date for those of
us who were privileged to be involved in organising the reunion of
716 Company RASC 6th Airborne Division for the rededication of the
Memorial Alms Dish.

Stanley, Gill, Janet and Judith are indebted to all of you who helped
to make this occasion so memorable and successful, whether helping in
the preparations beforehand or on Sunday helping at the Church and the
Hall. Wherever you helped, we thank you. Minstead village became a
unit and we worked amicably together to produce an outstandingly
successful day which was so appreciated by all our visitors.

We particularly thank Michael for giving us a truly special and moving
service. We are humble and proud to have been given the opportunity to
organise this reunion, but we could not have done it without your help.
Thank you.

> Minstead means a lot to 716 Company -
> 716 Company means a lot to Minstead.

The Memorial Alms Dish to fallen comrades remains with us to keep, to
treasure and to respect for all time.

STANLEY, GILL, JANET, JUDITH

ACKNOWLEDGEMENTS

My grateful thanks to:

SQUIRE CHRISTOPHER GREEN for agreeing that the Compton Coat of Arms be used at the front of this book.

GILLIAN, my wife, for her patience and support and for her initial proof reading of my longhand pages.

ANGELA GALES who undertook the Herculian task of interpreting my longhand notes and typing them for proofreading. She then produced the initial typed copy of the book. She has been responsible for the long-running task of liaising with the publisher regarding our editing and re-editing of proof copies.

JANE, my younger daughter, for researching any Copyright Holders of illustrations and informative notes printed in this book and obtaining any relevant permissions to use them.

BILL ANDREWS for writing Preface.

EMILY SPENCE for composing Foreword.

STEVE CATTELL for sourcing the dates on two house date plaques and for confirming details of the transfer of bells to Whitechapel.

GEOFFREY GREEN for detailing campanology at church and our visit to Whitechapel.

SOURCES

Photographs

Cattle Grid, Elm Road House – John Gibbons

Author 2018 – Robert Osborne

Author and Family 1967 – a Wantage neighbour

Buster and Me – Gillian Gibbons

All other photographs – by the Author

All diagrams and Nature Trail items – by the Author

Airborne Forces Prayer – no rights claimed by the existing Forces.

Facts quoted from letter to the Author by the late Billie Iremonger – no descendants traced.

Reminiscence – the history of "R.A.S.C. 716 Company, Light," by the late "Jock" Brennan quoted in part – no descendants traced.

The Author's thanks to all residents of Minstead still alive who replied to his 1975 request for information about the history of their properties.

The late Mrs Sybil White loaned original documents re "The 1921 Sale" to the Author for photocopying. These have been quoted.

The Author sincerely thanks the Service Manager for Legal Services of the present New Forest District Council for having no objection to the Author using and quoting from information relating to the history of Minstead properties supplied to the Author by the Legal Officer of the 1975 New Forest District Council.

N. B. All our attempts to trace copyright holders or their descendants have failed. We invite any copyright holders or their descendants to make themselves known to the publishers.